Psalms
Ancient Songs for These Times

Rabbi Yael Levy

A Way In
Philadelphia, Pennsylvania
awayin.org

Also by Rabbi Yael Levy

Directing the Heart: Weekly Mindfulness Teachings and Practices from the Torah

*Journey through the Wilderness: A Mindfulness Approach to the
Ancient Jewish Practice of Counting the Omer*

Published by:
A Way In
Philadelphia, PA
www.awayin.org

ISBN: 978-1-7332384-2-7 (Paperback)
ISBN: 978-1-7332384-3-4 (e-book)

Library of Congress Control Number: 2026903291

Cover photo: Yael Levy
Author's Photo: Nick Pilotta
Design: Susan Bowman

Table of Contents

Psalm 101

To the Beloved, a Psalm

I will sing of love and fairness;
I will offer melodies to you,
the Great Unfolding of All.

I will reflect on paths of integrity.
When will I understand how to walk in these ways?
I will practice in the depths of my heart.

I won't be led astray by distractions that appear before my eyes.
I will not allow hatred to cling to my thoughts.
I won't let viciousness take root in my heart.
I will not engage the wickedness that arises among us.

I won't abide the inclination to slander friends and neighbors in secret,
and I will be aware of arrogance as I seek to expand my heart.

My eyes are on the faithful of the land, to dwell with them by my side.
My guides will be those who walk with integrity.

I will not allow deception to live in my house.
Lies and dishonesty will not stand before my eyes.

Each morning, I will imagine wickedness vanishing from earth
and cities everywhere filled with the sacred presence of love.

A New Way of Seeing

It was about 20 years ago that the Psalms took me by surprise. I was already acquainted with these ancient songs that are central to Jewish liturgy; they had long been a part of my daily prayer practice. I had been carrying a Book of Psalms with me for quite a while, often turning to them for inspiration.

But in many ways, they still felt impenetrable.

Then in 2005, at our synagogue auction, I picked up a book called *The Divine Hours: Prayers for Autumn and Wintertime,* edited by Phyllis Tickle. The book is a contemporary rendition of the Book of Hours, a devotional Christian prayer book that guides the reader through prayers and intentions for five devotional hours of the day—pre-dawn, morning, mid-day, late afternoon, early evening and night. This particular volume was a guide for October through January.

I took the book home that autumn evening and decided to follow its journey through the following few months. I was astounded by what I found.

The prayers for the Daily Hours included hundreds of individual psalm verses. This was an entirely new way of encountering psalms for me. I was accustomed to reading whole psalms and working (and at times slogging) through long, difficult passages that often were harsh and confusing.

Here was an invitation to sit with a few verses from different psalms and let them linger. Even just one verse could be enough.

Many of the verses that I traveled with through those days were new to me. Others were familiar, but it felt as if I were encountering them for the first time.

Meeting the individual verses on their own in Tickle's raw, unabashed translations from the Hebrew invited an intimacy I had never before experienced. It felt as if the Divine were reaching for me, calling me to follow my longings for closeness. Presented this way, the psalm verses encouraged my vulnerability. As the authors of these ancient songs shouted with joy, begged for help or wept in despair, they burst through my self-consciousness and opened a way for me to cry out without feeling embarrassed.

I felt drawn into a surrender that was new, exciting and even frightening.

Inspired by the offerings of individual verses, I began a practice of opening the biblical Book of Psalms at random and reading through a full psalm slowly, listening for verses that spoke to my heart. I allowed myself to ignore my mind saying that I couldn't pick and choose, and paused with the verses that I found helpful. This deep listening was, in itself, a new practice.

Each morning I would sit with a verse in meditation. First, I would say the verse aloud, then silently repeat it again and again, returning to the verse each time I noticed my

attention had wandered. At times, I practiced sitting with
the same psalm verse for weeks. Other times, I looked for a
new verse each day.

This is such a regular practice for me now that it's hard to
remember how new and different it felt then. My prayer
life had been rooted in the prayers and structure of the
traditional liturgy. It felt radical to comb through a single
psalm, find a verse that called to me and to sit with just that
one line. And at that time, for me, it was.

This practice changed me. Over the days, months and years
since then, the Psalms have taken root and grown inside of
me. I have sat and walked with them, meditated and swum
with them. I have used them in my teaching and counseling.
They are part of the fabric of my life.

Sitting with psalm verses has helped create a foundation that
holds me when the world is shaking and I am reeling. Their
companionship offers solace and refuge. They shape my
faith and increase my courage. Their words turn me toward
gratitude, wonder and joy.

The Psalms continually call me back to relationship with
the Divine Source and remind me that, no matter what,
I am not alone. From the heart of mystery, the Psalms
urge me on.

Developing A Relationship

This book is about developing a relationship with the
Psalms: experiencing them as a guide, a companion and a
foundation for spiritual practice. It is an exploration of how
the Psalms can inspire and strengthen us, helping us live
with reverence, courage and care.

Arranged as a collage, it is made up of individual psalm
verses, translations of full psalms and instructions for
practice. Also included are teachings and stories from
my own experiences. The book can be read in the order
presented and you might find yourself exploring sections out
of order as well.

*

The Book of Psalms is a collection of 150 lyrical poems
found in the third section of the Hebrew Bible—*Ketuvim*,
Writings.

The word for psalm in Hebrew is *mizmor*, which means
jubilant song or melody. Most often, though, the Psalms are
called *t'hillim*, meaning to praise and to shine.

No one really knows who wrote the Psalms. Traditionally
they are all attributed to King David, or alternatively to
King David as well as to Moses, Solomon, the sons of
Korach and other named authors. However, many scholars
agree that the Psalms were composed by various anonymous

authors between 996 and 457 BCE. Certain psalms were sung as people ascended to the Temple and as they made their ritual offerings. Accompanied by musical instruments, psalms also enhanced communal celebrations outside of the Temple ritual.

After the destruction of the Second Temple in 70 CE, prayer replaced sacrifice, and the Psalms became part of daily liturgy. Particular psalms became associated with each day and with Shabbat celebrations and holiday observance.

I am content to have the question of who wrote the Psalms remain a mystery. It helps me to hear in these ancient texts the calls of each of us yearning for the sacred, united in celebration and sorrow.

The 150 Psalms represent a vast array of moods and perspectives. They sing of intimate relationship with God and the world, and they cry out into the loneliness of the abyss. They rejoice with abandon and wail in confusion. They tremble with rage and dread and sing with gratitude and delight. Sometimes they act as vehicles to help us travel from torment to hope. Always they illuminate the pain and joys of being alive.

A good friend reminded me that the Psalms don't strive for consistency. A Psalm will shout with joy in one verse and plead desperately for help in the next.

In Psalm 118, we hear:

> *This is the day the One has made;*
> *let us rejoice and delight in it.*
> Psalm 118:24

Then, immediately, the same Psalm calls:

> *Please save us, Infinite One, please;*
> *we beseech you.*
> Psalm 118:25

A Psalm may swing between points of view and arrive at a completely different place from where it began.

Psalm 13 opens with anguished cries:

> *Will you forget me forever, Divine Presence?*
> *How long will you hide from me?*
> *How long will my heart be filled with confusion and grief?*
> *How long will torment consume me?*
> Psalm 13:2–3

Just a few verses later, the Psalm closes with a declaration of relationship and joy:

> *And I trust in your abundant love.*
> *My heart rejoices in your expansive presence.*
> *I will sing into the Infinite Mystery,*
> *for all the good bestowed.*
> Psalm 13:6

In the rhythm of the Psalms, I hear an echo of my own
ricocheting emotions. The Psalms help me notice that
my thoughts often swing from joy to fear, desperation to
hope, gratitude to anger, in a matter of moments. And
rather than seeing this as a personal flaw, the Psalms help me
understand that this is a human response to the challenges
and blessings of life.

There are moments when I turn to a psalm and hear it speak
clearly. Other times, the text is so murky or feels so jarring, I
struggle to find meaning.

Always, I hear the Psalms call me to leap beyond the
rational. They urge me to engage my imagination and release
the need for everything to make perfect sense. In doing so,
they help me develop new ways to meet what life brings.

I hope you will find inspiration in these pages and feel
encouraged to create your own relationship with these
sacred, inconsistent texts.

As we give voice to them, these ancient songs call back to us,
meeting our longings with guidance and support.

Translations

I began translating psalms from the Hebrew many years ago
as a way to develop a deeper relationship with them. When
I do it for myself, it is a wondrous, fun practice. Over the
years, I have shared my translations with others in classes
and in my writings, but it still feels vulnerable to do so.

Each translation reflects my own experience with the psalm.
Each represents what I hear and yearn for at a particular
time. Each is an act of devotion.

At the best of times, I allow the psalm to speak and sing
without judging myself or the verses too harshly. Always,
I ask the question: *How can these words be helpful?*

Some of my translations stay very close to the Hebrew. Some
are more "in the vicinity," and at other times, they drift quite
far afield. They are, of course, my personal interpretations,
filtered through my life experiences.

There are some Hebrew words that I have been unable to
capture with one precise English equivalent. At various
times, I may translate the same Hebrew word differently
depending upon the context. In this book there are also
a few instances where I have translated a verse differently
when presenting it on its own and in its context within
a full psalm.

My translations are always in motion. I am constantly
making changes and, even with just slight variations, I
can feel the psalm come alive in a new way. I love this
constant becoming, and it is difficult to let go and allow the
translations to be still.

In this way, the Psalms teach me to create, to let go, to
soften my demand for perfection and to release some of the
grasping for getting it *just right.*

I bow to the probability that I will encounter these
translations at another time, be unhappy with some,
embarrassed or dissatisfied with others, and wish I had
translated them differently. (This has already happened many
times as I worked on this book).

For now, I sing along with the psalmist:

To you, Infinite Presence, I lift my soul.
May I trust
and not be ashamed.
Psalm 25:1–2

God
Who, What, Where, When is God?

In the experience of the psalmists, relationship with God was a given. At times, God's presence felt extremely close, deeply personal. At others, the Divine Presence seemed distant, hidden, utterly out of reach. But there never was a question for the psalmists that God was there, even when they couldn't see or fathom it.

In today's world, notions of God can disturb some and put off many, but I find the psalmist's intimacy with and longing for God so helpful. The Psalms call me into relationship with a force that is incomprehensible and also always present. They encourage me not to try to rationally explain this relationship, but rather to be daring and unashamed in my search for and awareness of the Divine. In sorrow, joy, fear, gratitude and celebration, the Psalms sing: God is here.

Psalms invite us into our own relationship with Divine Mystery. They urge us to persist even as doubts arise, even when we might feel ridiculous. Staying with the Psalms helps me break through my own skepticism. There are moments when psalms carry me into an expanse where I encounter the One.

*

In Jewish tradition, and in the Psalms, there are many names for God, each offering different visions and pathways for relationship. The two most traditional names for God are *Elohim* and the Hebrew letters *Yod-Heh-Vav-Heh.*

Elohim is the first name for God that appears in the Torah—in the story of creation, Genesis Chapter 1. *Elohim* is the force through which all life comes to be. I often translate it as *Divine Source, Life Force, Source of All.*

Yod-Heh-Vav-Heh: This name of God is considered unpronounceable, unknowable and so sacred that many refer to it as *Hashem*—literally, "the Name." In Hebrew it is often vocalized as *Adonai,* which means *my Lord.* The word *Adonai* has no intrinsic relationship to this sacred name, and I find it distracts from its meaning and mystery by giving rise to an image of a hierarchical God who judges and decrees.

The Hebrew letters *Yod-Heh-Vav-Heh* contain the word *to be*, an action—a verb—rather than a noun. It points to the process of Infinite Being and Infinite Becoming. This name dissolves any distinction between past, present and future, and points to an Unfolding Mystery that is here within every moment *and* beyond our grasp. I often translate this name as: *Infinite Presence, The One, or Unfolding Mystery.*

I have found that engaging with the various ways of referring to God changes my experience of the Divine. Using the words *Mystery, Life Force* and *Infinite Presence* has helped me move beyond my childhood image of a being who sits on a heavenly throne in judgment. It has encouraged me to feel God as a sacred presence, the very breath of life itself.

As you move through the Psalms, here are some names for the Divine to explore. Consider substituting one of these as you come across references to God.

Havayah: This name contains the letters of the unknowable name, Y-H-V-H, in a different order. It means *Being, the Life Force of All Existence.*

Shechina: The Indwelling Divine Presence

Rachamana: Compassionate One

Makom: Place; an affirmation that the Divine is right here, in this moment

Ruach: Spirit; Breath

Echad: One; Oneness

Tzur: Rock

Yah: A calling forth of *Yod-Hey-Vav-Heh*; Breath of All Life

An Angry God

Sometimes I open to a psalm and am startled anew by its depiction of an angry, vengeful God.

I am shaken by the image of a malevolent, jealous being who punishes us severely if we go astray.

While I continue to reject the Bible's depiction of a God who is brutal and vindictive, I do relate to the image of a Divine Force filled with fury. It reflects the rage that some political and social realities ignite in me.

I am so incensed by the cruelty and viciousness of our current leadership that, at times, the indignation seeps into my everyday encounters and I find myself fuming at the slightest provocation.

I realize that the anger I am experiencing might not abate any time soon. Instead of trying to dispel it, I need to learn how to allow the outrage while keeping it from becoming all there is. Can I harness this furious energy in ways that are helpful? Can it be directed toward healing?

I don't know.

For now, I am reluctant to let go of an angry God. Instead, I want a God to do battle for me—for us. I want a God to slay the evildoers, even though I don't believe this is who or what God is.

It is we humans who react with jealousy, who are vindictive
and seek power and control through fear and punishment.
These reactions belong in the human realm, not the Divine.

In the Psalms' depiction of Divine wrath, I choose to hear an
echo of the horror I feel as I witness violence and brutality.
In God's vengeful fury, I experience the rage that arises in
me as I see the proliferation of greed and cruelty. In God's
fierce fulminations, I am listening for a rage that is sacred.

I am burning with rage because of the wicked
who have abandoned the sacred teachings.
Psalm 119:53

May those who bring devastation be consumed by shame.
May those who pursue destruction perish,
covered in disgrace.
Psalm 71:13

The Battle

I live with so much noise: information streaming 24 hours a day, up-to-the-minute news, constant political and social commentary. And always more suggestions about things I need to buy.

Then there is the noise from my own mind: worries that loop around and won't let go, harsh judgments, stories that encourage fear and doubt.

Spiritual practices ground me, shift my perspective and keep me from being waylaid by all this commotion.

What is spiritual practice? Keeping it simple, a spiritual practice is an intentional activity that calms the mind, opens awareness, and brings us into deeper relationship with the movement and mysteries of life.

Spiritual practice can be prayer or meditation, of course, but it doesn't have to be. Our practices can include just about anything we do with devotion that helps focus our energy and attention—movement, gardening, cooking, knitting, making art and music, yoga, bird watching, hiking and so much more.

We can also view spiritual practice as the simple and complex act of paying attention and calling ourselves back to the present moment again and again.

No matter what the practice is, spiritual practice takes *practice*—and any activity to which we faithfully dedicate ourselves can strengthen us. In the language of Jewish tradition, practice requires both *keva* (structure) and *kavanah* (intention).

Keva calls us to do the practice even when we don't feel like it, to persist even when we feel distracted, rushed or uninspired. It reminds us that we need discipline to help the practices take root and become essential components of our daily lives.

Kavanah encourages us to approach our practices with heartfelt intention, to engage with curiosity and be open to what we will experience and discover. *Kavanah* also reminds us that our practices are meant to be enjoyed. It urges us not to try to twist ourselves into practices we don't like, but rather to choose one that comes naturally and includes things we love to do.

When designing a practice, it is helpful to:

Begin where we are and choose something that is not going to require huge, immediate changes.

Make a commitment to a practice that is doable. For example, when beginning a meditation practice, sit for a short time (5–10 minutes) for the first few weeks and gradually increase it.

Engage in the practice at a similar time each day. This
gets the mind and body accustomed to the practice, even
expecting it. After a while, you might even find the practice
calling to you.

There are days I step into my practice only out of a sense of
obligation, unwilling or unable to give it my full attention.
Other times, I embrace the practice with all I have. Even
when I don't feel like doing it and nothing much seems to
happen, I am always grateful that I took the time to pause
and engage.

At some point, resistance to practice is guaranteed to arise—
disinterest, annoyance, even anger. It is not always easy to
know when to push through the resistance and continue,
or when to listen to it and make changes. There is no
easy formula for discernment, but it always helps to meet
resistance with compassion, patience and curiosity. (This is
itself a great practice.)

> *May the fruits of our practice*
> *become our dwelling.*
> *May the seeds of our practice*
> *be the foundation for sacred relationship.*
> Psalm 102:29

Calling on the Psalms

I call upon the Psalms in prayer and meditation and I carry
verses with me throughout the day.

Psalm verses act as an antidote to the anxiety and fear that
often grab hold of me. They help shift my attention away
from scornful voices, harsh judgements and stories of
doom that my mind conjures. They replace these troubling
thoughts with images and concepts that bring calm and
sustenance.

I reach for psalms when I am confronting a difficult
situation. I call on them when I am spiritually exhausted and
when the world looks so bleak that I want to turn away.

I turn to psalms to help me give thanks, sing with delight
and marvel at the wonders of life.

I rely on them to help me reach toward Sacred Mystery.

I have discovered that I don't have to believe the message in
a psalm for the verse to be helpful. I just need to be diligent
about putting the verse into my system. I don't have to
believe, for example, that:

Infinite love fills all earth
Psalm 119:64

for this verse to be a beacon guiding me toward hope
and courage.

When I am feeling worn down or afraid, I don't have to feel
certain that:

I will walk in the presence of the One in the lands of life
Psalm 116:9

for this verse to inspire willingness and strength.

The Psalms revive me even when I pause with them for just a
few moments as I am going about my day.

Ideally, here is I what I do: As I notice the intrusive thoughts
and berating voices arise, I do my best to not engage
with them. I resist the urge to reason or argue them away.
Wrestling with them just gives them more energy, which
they certainly don't need.

Then I take a moment to name what is happening: *My
mind is spinning stories that are causing me to feel afraid. My
shoulders are tight, my stomach hurts. I am feeling anxious.* A
key here is to name this without judgment or blame.

Then I take a verse and repeat it over and over, using it as
a mantra. If I can concentrate on the meaning, that's great,
but not necessary. Just giving my mind something else to
focus on is tremendously helpful.

This practice demands persistence. Eventually, with effort
and repetition, the anxious thoughts recede, often for a quite
a while. Sometimes, though, the worries come rushing back

in. Even when this happens, I find that the verse has brought some comfort and relief. With practice, I have found that the psalm verses arise more easily and have greater impact.

It can be quite powerful to say a verse aloud. This may feel awkward at first, but when the phrase is given breath and sound, the psalm comes alive in a new way.

Verses for this practice can be:

A verse that asks for help:

> *Infinite Presence, let your abundant love reach me.*
> Psalm 119:41

A verse that sets an intention:

> *I place the Infinite Presence before me always.*
> Psalm 16:8

A verse that seeks support:

> *Be for me a sheltering rock to which I can always come.*
> Psalm 71:3

Or any verse that helps direct the attention and bring calm (even for a short while) to the noisy mind.

Meditation Practice

Many years ago, when I began a meditation practice, I was instructed to anchor my attention on the breath. I found this challenging. As soon as I would begin, my mind would start spinning with worries about the breathing itself: *I am not breathing deeply enough . . . My breath is too short, too shallow—something must be wrong.*

Try as I might, I could not quiet these fears.

What a relief it was, then, to give myself permission to bring psalm verses into my meditation. They became the focus for my attention, the place I would return when I noticed my mind wandering.

I still practice in this way. I meditate with a psalm, repeating it gently. Sometimes I choose a verse that offers comfort, support or inspiration. Other times, I choose a verse that helps me focus on a quality I want to cultivate in myself, or a verse that guides me in how I might best meet that moment's blessing or challenge.

Taking Psalms into Sitting Meditation

We take a seated posture and begin by reading the verse aloud.

Then, with eyes closed (or softly focused), we let the attention rest gently on the breath and repeat the verse silently.

Over and over, we slowly repeat the verse. It can be helpful
to feel the words travel with the movement of the breath.

Each time we notice that our attention has wandered (which
it will again and again), we give thanks for noticing and
return to the psalm verse.

At the end of the meditation, we once again say the verse
aloud.

This practice can be done with any verse that speaks to us.
It is helpful to choose a verse—or a part of a verse—that is
short enough to memorize.

When meditating with the Psalms, I find it beneficial to sit
with the same verse for a few weeks. This helps me form a
relationship with the text. After a while, the verse comes to
me with greater ease, and it usually reveals itself in new ways.

Of course, if you are sitting with a psalm verse and it doesn't
feel right, make a change.

Some of my most faithful companions for meditation
practice are:

I am my prayer to you.
Psalm 69:14

To You, Infinite Presence,
I lift my soul.
Psalm 25:1

I trust in the Infinite Unfolding.
Psalm 31:15

I choose the path of faith.
Psalm 119:30

*

This book is filled with verses from the Psalms. They are arranged thematically in the hope that they will offer guidance for different moments in our lives. Many verses could fit into any number of categories and they all, in some way, transcend categorization.

As you engage with the psalm verses, give yourself permission to notice where they take you, what images arise, where you feel most drawn. Sing them, journal with them, let them inspire your art.

Be surprised by them.

Giving Thanks

I direct my heart toward gratitude.
Psalm 119:7

The day before I was to lead one of my first Jewish
Mindfulness retreats, my son got into trouble at school.
This set off a tumultuous evening as I dealt with the
ramifications. Things were still unresolved when, the next
morning, I got up very early to take a walk in the woods. My
thoughts were reeling.

*What a mess this is. How can I possibly lead a retreat with all
this happening?*

Then, surprisingly, I heard, or maybe just felt, a call to give
thanks. This made little sense to me; I did not feel grateful.
But the call, wherever it came from, persisted: give thanks
anyway.

So I did. I yelled out, "Thank you, thank you, thank you—
OK, already—thank you."

After laughing at how ridiculous I felt (and probably
appeared), I looked around, taking notice of where I was:
tall trees, luminous sky. I gave thanks. I thanked the trees,
the rocks, the ground under my feet. I thanked the birds, my
dog. I thanked the early morning light.

As I continued, something lifted. I felt lighter, not as
besieged. I still had to deal with a very distressing situation,
but I didn't feel so alone. Dare I say, I even felt thankful.

Psychological research confirms what I experienced in the woods that day: noticing things to be grateful for and expressing thanks significantly changes our brains. Gratitude strengthens our capacity to deal with difficult situations, reduces worry and increases calm. Giving thanks calls us present and shifts our attention away from recriminations about the past or unease about the future.

Psalms can help us turn toward gratitude. It's my practice to say verses of thanksgiving each day, no matter how grateful I feel—or don't feel. Over time, I have found that these offerings act as a balm for dread and anxiety.

Who, what am I thanking? I don't really know.

Many psalm verses direct our gratitude toward God, the mysterious Infinite Presence beyond and within all creation.

I give thanks to you, Infinite Mystery, with all my heart.
Psalm 9:2

Sometimes I direct my gratitude toward a "you" that is less defined:

I bow into the holy
and give thanks for all that manifests,
for love, for truth.
Psalm 138:2

Sometimes I give thanks without directing it anywhere specific:

In the middle of the night,
I rise and give thanks.
Psalm 119:62

What If We Can't Feel Grateful?

Many of us experience times of tremendous grief or tragedy, when gratitude feels impossible to reach and the call to give thanks only adds more pain. At these times, it is enough to acknowledge the situation, to be present to it.

The Hebrew word for gratitude, *hoda'ah*, means both thankfulness and acknowledgement.

When acknowledgement is all we can do, it is important to not berate ourselves. We can use the Psalms to help us be right where we are, substituting *I am present to* for *I give thanks.*

I am present to this moment with all my heart.
Psalm 86:12

To you,
I make an offering of my presence.
In the name of the Infinite Mystery, I call out.
Psalm 116:17

Our willingness to call ourselves present to whatever we are experiencing is a powerful offering.

Practicing

In establishing a gratitude practice, you might adopt a psalm verse to say when you feel grateful and another when gratitude feels beyond reach.

You can repeat a verse of gratitude to begin or end the day—or both.

You might notice how it feels to say a verse with and without a direct object:

I give thanks to you with all my heart.
Psalm 138:1

or

I give thanks with all my heart.
Psalm 138:1

Let the verse and the moment gently guide you.

Verses for Giving Thanks

Let us give thanks into the Unfolding Mystery for all the good.
Love and generosity are forever.
Psalm 118:1

I give such thanks to the Infinite Presence.
In the midst of multitudes,
I offer praise.
Psalm 109:30

I give thanks to you with all my heart.
In relationship with the Divine source, I sing.
Psalm 138:1

I give thanks into hidden mystery.
Psalm 52:11

It is good to offer thanks into the Infinite Unfolding,
to sing
and reach for the heights.
Psalm 92:2

Halleluyah
With all my heart, I give thanks into the Unfolding Mystery,
in intimate circles,
and within sacred community.
Psalm 111:1

Free my soul from prison that I might give thanks.
Psalm 142:8

I give thanks
for I am awesomely and wondrously made.
Psalm 139:14

We give thanks to you, Source of All, we give thanks.
Your presence is so close.
Psalm 75:2

Give thanks into the Unfolding Mystery,
with music,
with song.
Psalm 33:2

Sorrow . . . And Joy

Serve the One in awe;
rejoice in trembling.
Psalm 2:11

One year in my annual struggle to bring forth a teaching that was worthy to be offered on *Kol Nidre* (Yom Kippur eve), the most sacred night of the year, I simply could not find anything to say. Every path I explored led nowhere.

During a conversation with a trusted friend, I realized why. I was feeling so much hurt and sadness about what was happening in our country and world, and I was using all my energy to deny these feelings. I was afraid that if I touched the sorrow, I would be swallowed by despair. If I really allowed the anguish, I would drown in it.

I understood then that, in order to have something authentic to say on Yom Kippur, I needed to surrender and feel the fullness of my grief. When I did, it felt like the sorrows had no end.

Yet as I continued to allow myself to dwell in the distress, something shifted. The hurt softened my heart somehow and I saw that the sadness was actually rooted in love.

Underneath the misery was my love for earth, trees, creatures of the wild. Underneath the pain was my love for this country and its hope and promise. Underneath the heartache was my love for people throughout the world that I don't even know.

I realized that, in turning toward sorrow, I was also turning toward all that I cherish. Allowing my heart to break open brought me close to all that I cared about.

While that sorrow persists, it isn't—as I feared—all there is. Instead, the love I touch opens me to beauty, kindness and connection. And to my surprise, it encourages me to find joy in the simplest moments:

The taste of a great cup of tea.
Watching birds sail across the sky.
A friend reaching out a hand to help me over slippery rocks.

Joy, I have come to realize, is a spiritual practice, one that can be hard to maintain as thoughts protest:

How can I be joyful when so much lies in ruin?
I might feel joy now, but something bad is sure to happen.
Hurry, there is work to be done. There is no time to pause and delight.

Joy is fuel, nourishment, sustenance. It gives us energy and strength—and brings front and center all that is worthwhile in this fragile and precious life. Joy encourages us to keep rising for what we love and value. It is a *mitzvah*, a sacred act, to seek out gladness, to sing and dance in delight.

Psalms can help us both celebrate and grieve.

They are with us when we are in the depths of despair:

Filled with anguish, I seek the Presence.
I stretch out my hands.
I weep at night. I cannot stop.
My soul refuses comfort.
Psalm 77:3

I cry out to the Source of All, my Rock.
Why have you forgotten me?
Why do I walk alone in darkness,
anguished and afraid?
Psalm 42:10

They urge us to fully embrace delight:

Come into the Sacred Presence with thanksgiving.
Let us sing out in joy; let us shout in delight.
Psalm 95:2

I celebrate the works of creation.
I shout for joy at the magnificence that unfolds.
Psalm 92:5

These days, joy feels like an act of defiance. Knocked down by wreckage and pain, we continue to rise, we continue to celebrate.

Certainly, there are times I have been unable to rise. I feel worn out, despondent. And there are moments that I have been able to let go into the fullness of joy. Dancing with friends, letting the music lift me as I sing along, watching the setting sun turn the waters of a lake pink, orange and gold, I am filled to overflowing.

As we go about our days, let us be gentle toward ourselves and each other as joy turns into sorrow and sadness makes way for delight.

In the evening, I lay down weeping;
then dawn brings songs of joy.
Psalm 30:6

You turned my mourning into dancing.
You loosened my grief and I was clothed in delight.
Psalm 30:12

The next chapter includes verses from the Psalms that call out in sorrow and in joy.

Cries of Sorrow

My soul dissolves in grief.
Please sustain me.
Psalm 119:28

The Infinite One is close to the brokenhearted.
In our crushed spirits, the One is present.
Psalm 34:19

Listen to our anguished cry;
make our hearts firm.
Hear us.
Psalm 10:17

Be gracious to me, Infinite One,
see my torment.
Lift me up from the gates of death.
Psalm 9:14

Torn open, the earth quakes.
Heal her brokenness.
Psalm 60:4

Arise, Infinite Presence,
lift up your hand.
Do not forget our anguish and despair.
Psalm 10:12

Infinite Presence, why are you so distant,
hidden in such troubled times?
Psalm 10:1

Infinite Mystery, hear my voice when I call.
Please, guard my life from terror and dread.
Psalm 64:2

Hear my prayers, Sacred Mystery, listen to my cries.
Do not be silent as I weep.
Psalm 39:13

The Infinite One heals our broken hearts
and holds us in our sorrows.
Psalm 147:3

Shouts Of Joy

This is the moment the Mystery has made:
let us rejoice and delight in it.
Psalm 118:24

Singing and dancing, we shout,
Our wellspring is in you.
Psalm 87:7

Raise a shout to the Infinite Mystery, all earth;
break through in joyous song.
Psalm 98:4

Seek the Presence with joy and delight.
Psalm 70:5

I rejoice and celebrate you, Infinite Presence,
singing melodies to the Most High.
Psalm 9:3

How good it is to give thanks, to joyously sing into the Mystery.
Psalm 92:2

Bring joy to our sacred service,
for to you I lift my soul.
Psalm 86:4

Let the heavens rejoice,
let the earth delight.
Let the sea in its fullness roar.
Psalm 96:11

May my meditations bring sweetness into the Mystery.
I will rejoice in the One.
Psalm 104:34

Let our hearts rejoice in the Unfolding Mystery.
In the sacred presence, we trust.
Psalm 33:21

Let all who seek you find joys and delights.
Let them always say,
How loving is the expansive presence of the One.
Psalm 40:17

Sing a new song;
celebrate the good with shouts of joy.
Psalm 33:3

Awake, my soul, awake.
With music I will awaken the dawn.
Psalm 57:9

I will sing with sacred strength.
I will sing joyously to the morning,
for your infinite love has been my haven,
my refuge in times of trouble.
Psalm 59:17

You, Sacred Presence, put joy in my heart.
Psalm 4:8

Trust In The Unfolding

It was 2010, and I had negotiated with my congregation to take a sabbatical from June through October, which would mean I would be away for Rosh Hashanah and Yom Kippur. This was a very generous gift from the community—and a very big deal for me. I had been leading High Holy Day services for 19 years and, not only was I exhausted by their demands, I had lost a sense of what these holy days meant for me.

By then, I had been working with individual psalm verses for a while. As I began my sabbatical, I decided to choose one verse to guide my much-anticipated journey. Not only would I meditate with the verse each day, I would hold it up as a beacon to define and shape my time and experience.

I had a mindfulness kayak retreat in Alaska to look forward to in August, and a backpacking and camping trip in southeastern Utah that would span the Holy Days of Rosh Hashanah, Yom Kippur and Sukkot.

I chose as my guide a verse from Psalm 37 that I loved and was hoping to live into. At that time, I translated it as:

> *May I trust in the Unfolding Mystery and meet it well.*
> *May I dwell in the land and be nourished by its faith.*
> Psalm 37:3[1]

------

[1] My translations of psalm verses change over the years. Today I hear this verse as: *Trust in the Infinite Mystery and act for good. Dwell in the land and be nourished by faith*

It seems naïve now, but as I chose the verse, I was certain about how this Psalm would guide me. I would trust in and learn from the unfolding experiences of being in the wild. I would dwell with God in the vast waters of Alaska and in the red rock canyons of Utah. I would learn to meet well the challenges and opportunities of being in the wilderness, and I would be nourished by these sacred lands.

. . . Two weeks after my sabbatical began, my beloved Uncle Marty was diagnosed with Stage 4 lung cancer. He was not expected to live long. My uncle and I had been extraordinarily close. Only 17 years older than I, he was a confidant and friend. My mom, his sister, had also died of lung cancer 13 years earlier, so not only was I shaken to the core by this news, I also had a sense of the harrowing nature of the journey ahead.

My first response was to rage at the psalm verse—and at God: *This was not what I meant when I chose to Trust in the Unfolding Mystery. This was not what I wanted to have to meet well. This was certainly not the wilderness I asked to enter and be shaped by.* I felt like a child stamping my feet and crying at the unfairness of it all. I had been tricked and deceived by the Psalm and by God.

Fortunately, through a mixture of desperation, grace and the discipline of practice, I did not abandon the Psalm or my commitment to allow it to guide my days. Instead, I walked with it in the woods of the Wissahickon watershed near my Philadelphia home. I sat with it. I held it in front of me day and night. I brought it to the wilds of Alaska and to my uncle's bedside in what turned out to be his final weeks.

The Psalm was with me as I officiated at his funeral and sat with my family in our shared grief. It was with me as we got up from shiva on *erev* Rosh Hashanah and as I walked the back country canyons on Yom Kippur.

The Psalm verse humbled me. It took me beyond my expectations and illusions of control. It held up mystery and offered companionship. It redefined wilderness and helped me see the sacred wild in unwelcome and difficult situations.

Over the days and months, the Psalm verse became not just a guide, but also a shield. It was a protector and place of refuge. Even when I was too distraught to reach for it, somehow it was always there.

This is some of what I heard:

Trust in the Unfolding Mystery and meet it well.

Practice trusting that you are not alone, even when it feels like you are. Practice trusting that the Divine Presence is with you, even though things are not as you had hoped.

Practice being present. Practice responding to whatever the moment brings, with compassion and patience.

Dwell with the land and be nourished by its faith.

Walk slowly among the trees and listen. Be with canyons, skies and water. Don't try to make anything happen; allow the mystery to unfold.

Be nourished by relationships, by simple moments of connection, and by earth's endurance and generosity.

This Psalm verse was such a powerful guide that I continue to say it to this day. It is the verse at the heart of *A Way In Jewish Mindfulness Organization*, where I serve.

Psalms speak to each of us differently and they reveal themselves to us in new ways as time and circumstances unfold. I have learned that, even as I approach a psalm with a particular intention and a clarity about what I hear it saying, the Psalms will always surprise me and teach me something unexpected and new. This is their power.

Asking For Help

Be not far from me, for trouble is close, and I need your help.
Psalm 22:12

As a congregational rabbi, I often met with people who would do practically anything but ask others for help.

I know how they feel. For a long time, I too believed that it was better to do things on my own. I thought that asking for help was a sign of weakness that revealed character flaws. If someone asked for my help, I would gladly offer it, but I found it hard to be the one doing the asking.

Over time, I have come to see more clearly that we don't do anything on our own. Everything we eat, wear, rely on—all that sustains us—is the result of someone's help.

After some years, I grew to accept that it was OK to ask for help when I was sick or injured—but even then, I would hesitate, asking only a very small circle of family and friends.

It has taken a lot of practice to learn to ask for help even when I am not in dire straits. In doing so, I have discovered that it strengthens and expands my relationships. Revealing vulnerability and reaching out deepens my connection with others. It has been an important lesson to see how asking someone for help offers them the opportunity to feel needed, valued. How great to be able to feel that we are useful and of service.

But asking *God* for help? Calling out *help me* into the vastness of the universe? That's something else entirely.

On one of my backpacking trips in the Utah desert, I got very lost. I thought I was paying attention, noticing the turns of the canyon, when suddenly I realized I could not find my way back to camp.

I panicked. I began to trip over rocks looking for the trail. I berated myself for wandering off. I lashed out at the silent desert. Out of desperation, I began crying out for help. "Help me, help me, help me please," I shouted aloud. "Please, please, help me," I called over and over again.

The crying out settled me somehow. It helped me stand still and look around without being completely besieged by terror. Finally, after what felt like a very long time—but was probably only about 15 minutes—I noticed a rock cairn that showed me the way back to camp.

I have cried out for help for years now. I still do every day. I call out not with the expectation that a divine hand is going to miraculously deliver the outcome or assistance I am pleading for.

I cry out for help because it calms my fright and despair. It loosens the constriction of dread and brings relief, even if only for a few moments.

Calling out reminds me that I don't have to figure out everything by myself. And sometimes the calling opens me to guidance that comes from within or appears in surprising, unexpected ways.

During these days of horrendous political and social upheaval, I have been calling out for help often. It is a balm for my tender and troubled heart.

Even as I don't see the results I long for, somehow the calling, the pleading, the asking, brings a moment of connection that carries comfort and offers tiny glimmers of hope.

On the next pages are psalm verses that cry out for help. Try calling these verses aloud.

Many are in the singular. You might want to practice moving between the singular and the plural (help me/help us) and see how it feels.

Calling Out For Help

Hear me, please, Infinite One,
be gracious with me.
Please, be my help.
Psalm 30:11

I am in distress and in so much need.
God, come to me quickly.
You are my help;
please hurry.
Psalm 70:6

Send forth your help from the holy realms,
your support from sacred places.
Psalm 20:3

Help us, God, please, for the sake of all that is.
Psalm 79:9

Help me, Infinite Presence,
save me with your generous love.
Psalm 109:26

My help comes from the Infinite Mystery,
revealed in the heavens and earth.
Psalm 121:2

Send forth your light and truth;
they will guide me.
Psalm 43:3

When I feel myself falter,
your love supports me.
In the midst of anxiety and dread,
your comfort soothes my soul.
Psalm 94:18-19

Let me see that the Source of All is my help,
the Infinite Mystery my support.
Psalm 54:6

From the narrow place,
I call out to the One
and I am answered with expansiveness.
Psalm 118:5

The Infinite calls: I am the One who lifts you
out of constriction and fear.
Make yourself wide and I will fill you.
Psalm 81:11

Send your burdens to the Infinite Presence.
The Presence will sustain us
and not let us fall.
Psalm 55:23

Call upon me in times of trouble.
I will help you.
This will honor me.
Psalm 50:15

As We Begin The Day

The beginning of wisdom is yirat hashem,
awe of the Infinite Unfolding Mystery.
Psalm 111:10

Jewish tradition teaches that this is the first psalm verse we
are to say each morning. I have been doing this practice
for a long time, and it has become a foundation stone. It
reminds me that I am not the source of wisdom. Insight and
understanding come from the realm of mystery. My role is
to bow in awe and allow wisdom to be revealed.

The word *awe* in Hebrew, *yirah*, indicates both wonder
and fear.

Yirah as wonder calls forth a practice of radical amazement.
It urges us to:
Look at the world with curiosity.
See the marvels.
Notice the spectacular in the everyday.
Let our hearts cry, *Wow.*

Yirah as fear calls us to:
Tremble at the great mysteries of life and death.
Quake as we stare into the unknown.
Shudder at all that is beyond human control.

Yirah as fear is not encouraging us to be afraid of
punishment. It is not calling us to be frightened that if we
do something wrong, we will be harshly disciplined by a
mighty heavenly force.

Rather, it is teaching us to fear what happens when we humans deny mystery and act as if we are the source of all knowledge and wisdom. We should fear what happens when we fail to recognize our interdependence with all life. Ignoring our intricate relationships with earth, each other, and all creatures enables us to justify actions that cause immense harm.

> *The beginning of wisdom is awe*
> *of the Infinite Unfolding Mystery.*
> Psalm 111:10

See wonders.
Bow to Mystery.
Act for the benefit of all.

Placing Love On My Heart

*Your infinite love is before my eyes, and I will walk
in the truths revealed.*
Psalm 26:3

Those who know me well are amazed at my impatience. Recently, after a frustrated tirade about heavy traffic and the ineptitude of so many drivers, my partner turned to me and asked, "Aren't you a mindfulness rabbi?"

I took a moment to consider the question. "Yes," I said, "and this is me with 25 years of practice."

I am aware of how easily I turn toward contention—how much I love to be right. And even as I sometimes enjoy the momentary pleasure of all this righteousness, it is not who I want to be.

I turn to psalm verses to guide me in cultivating the qualities I want to live into.

During the day, as I find myself growing frustrated or weary with someone or something, I say to myself:

Your infinite love is before my eyes, and I will walk in the truths revealed.

I call on this verse to lift me beyond my limitations and connect me with a love that is much greater than anything I could ever generate. I carry it with me as a way to cultivate

the capacity to meet the world with generosity and respond
to what I encounter with patience and understanding.

Lately, I've had trouble turning to this verse and others
like it that declare that the Divine overflows with infinite,
steadfast love. *Look at this world,* my heart cries—*so much
devastation and cruelty. Where is love in all this wreckage?*

Your infinite love is before my eyes.

I persist with this verse.

I place it upon my heart so the anger I feel at what we
humans have wrought does not take root in my soul and
grow into hatred.

I repeat it over and over because I want to be a person who
can see the world in its beauty and ruin—and continue to
walk in the ways of love.

Uncertainty

Many years ago, I was walking on the beach with my Uncle Marty, marveling at the light on the ocean and talking about life, as we would.

I was fearful about decisions I needed to make concerning work and home—worried about what might unfold from pursuing different options. Would I choose the right path? Would events I couldn't imagine interfere with what I hoped would be?

My Uncle Marty, with his exuberant love, turned to me, arms spread wide and said, "When nothing is known, anything is possible."

Not knowing wasn't an obstacle; on the contrary, it was the source of great opportunity.

I have been returning to that moment a lot lately—to the call of the ocean, to my uncle's love, to my youthful innocence, to the adventurous hope I felt. And to his words: *When nothing is known, anything is possible.*

These days, much of what my mind thinks it knows about what will happen in this country, in the world and to our planet, is harrowing.

These "certainties" are unwelcome, to say the least—and I have to remind myself that, actually, I don't know.

I find it helpful to remember that the mind, so uncomfortable with *not knowing*, will grasp for certainty by creating story after story about what the future will bring—and most often, these scenarios will be filled with foreboding.

While uncertainty can feel destabilizing—and it can sound naïve to declare *I don't know* in the face of such turmoil and destruction —this is actually where I find hope.

Asserting *I don't know* challenges the horror stories that my mind insists upon. It calls me back to the present moment and enhances my ability to act.

There have been times when practicing *I don't know* that I have experienced a flash of awareness: we are all part of a great unfolding mystery, and anything—anything — can happen. Peace *can* be found. Justice *can* prevail. Broken relationships *can* be mended. Healing *is* possible.

And, *I don't know.*

In some moments now, I am able to appreciate uncertainty and even experience it as a blessing.

As I continue to wrestle with all that unfolds, psalm verses
offer support and encouragement:

They call me not to turn away:

They return me to the awareness of sacred mystery:

On the next pages are more psalm verses to help us draw
close to the sacred as we sit with uncertainty and possibility.

Verses For Drawing Close

With all my heart, I seek you.
Psalm 119:10

I will sing to the Infinite with my life.
I will make music with all that I am.
Psalm 104:33

May my prayers be rooted.
May they rise like incense.
May the offerings of my hands be received as a gift.
Psalm 141:2

Open my eyes that I might behold wonders.
Psalm 119:18

I am a sojourner with you.
Like all my ancestors,
I seek a place to dwell.
Psalm 39:13

Source of all, you are my God.
My soul thirsts for you, my flesh longs for you
like a parched and weary land without water.
Psalm 63:2

Infinite Presence, I am my prayer to you.
Psalm 69:14

In generosity, I will make my offering
and give thanks into the Infinite Unfolding
for all the good.
Psalm 54:8

Here I am. I have come with the scroll of the book
that is written upon me.
My greatest desire is to live in alignment with the Highest Will,
to live the wisdom placed deep within me.
Psalm 40:8-9

I enter your presence, raising up my offerings.
I make whole my vows.
Psalm 66:13

Bless the Divine Mystery, my soul.
Bless the vastness of the Great Unfolding.
Bless the splendor and radiance.
Behold the Mystery wrapped in light,
stretched across the arch of the skies.
Psalm 104:1-2

I lift my hands to do mitzvot;
I lift my hands to love.
Psalm 119:48

Truly you are my rock, my deliverance,
my haven.
I will not be shaken.
Psalm 62:7

In my integrity, I am supported.
In alignment, I stand in the presence of hidden mystery.
Psalm 41:13

May my mouth speak wisdom.
May the meditations of my heart
be for understanding.
Psalm 49:4

Source of All,
create in me a pure heart.
Renew in me a steadfast spirit.
Psalm 51:12

In your great love, I enter your house.
I lay myself down in your holy presence in awe.
Psalm 5:8

Tzedek – Justice

Open for me gates of justice;
I will enter and give thanks.
This is the gateway to the Infinite Presence.
Let all those seeking justice come in.
Psalm 118:19-20

The Psalms, like so many Jewish texts, call out for justice—
in Hebrew, *Tzedek.*

Sacred Mystery, answer us with awesome acts of justice.
Psalm 65:6

They command us to pursue justice:

We are called to act for justice, grounded in deep faith.
Psalm119:138

I grew up with the privilege of believing that justice was
surely possible. I felt safe in my family and community and
I had the freedom and opportunity to explore and grow. At
a young age, I watched the Nixon administration fall.
I witnessed a president, vice president and cabinet members
resign in disgrace.

My family's connection to Judaism was rooted in the call:
"With liberty and justice for all." Conversations around our
holiday table were focused on current events. I was taught to
believe that, with enough perseverance and commitment, we
could make the world a more just place.

My family didn't deny our country's legacy of injustice and oppression; rather, they believed we must help build a world of freedom, fairness, and equality.

I miss this innocence. I miss this hopeful clarity.

Like many of us, I am deeply shaken by the cruelty and deceit that comprise much of our social and political landscape. It is hard for me to imagine that justice will prevail—*can* prevail. And yet, I have to believe that what we do matters, that our words and actions—the ways we give of our time, resources and energy—make a difference.

> *Make offerings for justice*
> *and trust in the Infinite Presence.*
> Psalm 4:6

The call for *Tzedek,* for justice, is a call for active participation. It commands us to not give up because the work seems insurmountable. Acts of compassion, honesty and generosity can change the world—and us.

> *We will not turn away.*
> *We will live*
> *and call out on behalf of all.*
> Psalm 80:19

The work of *Tzedek* demands that we take the longest possible view—to know that no matter what we do, we might not see the world we long for in our lifetime. We are urged to act anyway, to strive for justice and peace, unattached to results.

Tzedek calls us to reach for strength from the Divine Mystery
and keep rising again and again for the sake of all life.

For the sake of my siblings, cousins and friends, I speak for peace.
For the sake of creation, I act for the well-being of all.
Psalm 122:8-9

Following are more psalm verses that cry out for *Tzedek*,
justice.

Calling For Justice

Let the mountains lift up peace for all;
let the hills raise up justice.
Psalm 72:3

Through justice, I will awaken to the Divine Presence.
Psalm 17:15

As you seek justice,
shout with joy into the Unfolding Mystery.
Sing, make music and praise.
Psalm 33:1

The world is filled with so much contempt.
Have mercy on us, Source of All.
Have mercy.
Psalm 123:3

Divine Presence, do not be silent, do not be still, do not be quiet,
for brutality rages and hatred lifts up its head.
Psalm 83:2-3

Love and truth meet.
Justice and peace embrace.
Truth sprouts from earth.
Justice gazes from the heavens.
Psalm 85:11-12

Light is sown through acts of justice,
joy through a steadfast heart.
Psalm 97:11

Let them sing and rejoice,
those who desire justice.
Let them say again and again,
Glorious is the Infinite Mystery,
who desires our service for the sake of shalom.
Psalm 35:27

Justice and fairness are your foundation.
Steadfast love and truth stand before you.
Psalm 89:15

Great peace comes to all who follow the teachings of love.
Psalm 119:165

I was struck silent by devastation and pain;
I could see no good.
My heart was raging within me;
my thoughts were a blazing fire.
Finally, I spoke out.
Psalm 39:3-4

Do good, Divine Presence, through seekers of good.
Come through our directed hearts.
Psalm 125:4

With hearts supported by the Infinite,
we will not be afraid.
In time we will see
tyrants fall.
Psalm 112:8

Infinite Presence,
may your abiding love come through me.
Psalm 119:41

May greed and arrogance no longer rule the earth.
May wickedness be no more.
Send blessings into the Unfolding Mystery, my soul;
I bend my knees, I offer praise.
Halleluyah
Psalm 104:35

Turn from evil and do good.
Seek peace;
pursue peace.
Psalm 34:15

The power of tyrants will be broken.
The Unfolding Mystery supports those who seek justice.
Psalm 37:17

Those seeking justice will rejoice.
They will celebrate in the presence of the Source;
they will be filled with delight and jubilation.
Psalm 68:4

I remember that your justice is beyond time and space.
This brings me comfort.
Psalm 119:52

We will build this world with love.
Psalm 89:3

Evil And Wickedness

For a long time, I turned away from psalm verses that
focus on evil and call for the wicked to be punished. These
passages felt harsh, angry and filled with a hatred that I did
not want to take into my system.

> *Traps of scorching fire*
> *will rain down upon the wicked,*
> *and a sulfurous wind will be their lot.*
> Psalm 11:6

I did not want to believe in evil. Even though I know that
we humans are capable of much violence and brutality, I
hesitated to describe anyone as wicked.

Now I am startled to find myself drawn to these passages.
In a time of such cruelty, when our world is on the brink of
tyranny, I need a battle cry that these psalm verses provide.

> *Rise up, Divine Presence, save us.*
> *Strike down the enemies of justice and decency.*
> *Shatter the wicked.*
> Psalm 3:8

These ancient songs give voice to my ache for justice. They
express my desire that the perpetrators of viciousness and
deceit be thwarted.

There is no shortage of psalms that allow me to feel rage and declare my longing that those who act with depraved cruelty face dire consequences:

The wicked, in their arrogance, pursue the most vulnerable.
May they be caught in the schemes they devise.
Psalm 10:2

Let those who seek to destroy
turn back in shame and confusion.
Let them be humiliated and disgraced.
Psalm 70:3

Though the wicked sprout like grass
and the evildoers blossom,
it is only that they may perish forever.
Psalm 92:8

How long, Infinite Presence,
how long will tyranny triumph?
Psalm 94:3

May those who seek to destroy plunge to the depths of earth.
May they be felled by the sword;
may they be prey to jackals.
Psalm 63:10-11

Break the power of the wicked and evil
so that, when we look,
tyranny will be not be found.
Psalm 10:15

Rescue me from tyrants;
save me from their violence and brutality.
Psalm 140:2

The tyrants draw their swords and bend their bows
to take down the poor and destitute,
to slaughter those on an upright path.
Their swords will pierce their own hearts.
Their bows will shatter.
Psalm 37:14-15

Please do not let my heart yield to evil.
Keep me from acting with malice.
I am surrounded by ruthless cruelty;
help me not give into these ways.
Psalm 141:4

Turn from evil and do good,
and you will dwell with eternity.
Psalm 37:27

I am saddened that this is the world I find myself in and dismayed by my angry response. I am grateful to the psalmists who remind me that I am not alone.

Choosing

I choose the path of faith and place practices before me.
Psalm 119:30

I say this verse every morning to help shape the way I walk
in the world.

There are days I awake filled with love and amazement. I feel
myself part of an infinite web of existence, in relationship
with all life. Other days, my mind gets caught in a snare of
dread and all I can see is ruin.

So, I choose the path of faith.

I choose to live in relationship with a sacred force that is
beyond my understanding. I choose to remember that my
perception is limited. I may not be able to see or imagine
how the world can be healed, but that does not mean it can't
happen.

I choose the path of faith.

I choose to bow to mystery and act with strength and
determination even when circumstances present so many
reasons to despair.

I choose to be guided, to walk with reverence and believe in
something that is beyond my understanding.

Sometimes I say this verse and feel it so deeply. Other times, any semblance of faith is beyond my reach.

I place practices before me.

When faith feels distant, or even ridiculous, I continue to say this verse again and again.

No matter how loud the distressing rants of my mind, I continue to turn to the Psalms and spiritual practice to fuel my devotion and make firm my steps.

Walking With Psalms

I love walking in the woods, and it is amazing that
sometimes, afterwards, I don't remember anything I saw
or felt. My mind had been so busy making plans, worrying
about something real or imagined, that I missed the
whole walk.

Again, I turn to the Psalms for help.

When I notice that my mind is distracted and I am not
paying attention to where I am, I say a psalm verse aloud
to call myself back. I repeat the verse again and again.
Sometimes I say it with great intention and other times
I just call it aloud without much feeling. It doesn't seem to
matter how I begin, because as I persist in the call, there
is usually a moment when something shifts. Trees, plants,
rocks and birds come back into focus. The psalm verse has
helped me return.

Of course, my mind will continue to wander and I will have
to keep calling myself back. But when I remember and am
willing to do this practice, I walk slower, experience more of
my surroundings, and return from the walk more refreshed.

Any psalm verse that speaks to you is great for this practice.
What follows are verses about walking our paths.

May I have the understanding to cherish the journey
and care for it with all my heart.
Psalm 119:34

Teach me the ways of Mystery.
I will walk in paths of truths;
unify my heart to live in awe.
Psalm 86:11

I will walk in the presence of the One in the lands of life.
Psalm 116:9

The Infinite Mystery leads us on our path,
helps direct our steps,
so we can find a place to settle.
Psalm 107:7

I will walk in a wide expanse seeking your teachings.
Psalm 119:45

The Mystery calls,
I give you good sense and fill you with light
so you can discern the path to walk.
Psalm 32:8

You have revived my deadened soul;
you have kept my feet from stumbling,
so that I may walk in the Divine Presence
in the light of life.
Psalm 56:14

I will travel pathways of connection,
for you have expanded my heart.
Psalm 119:32

As I begin the day,
let me be aware of your generous love.
I trust in you.
Help me know the paths to walk,
for to you I lift my soul.
Psalm 143:8

Songs That Yearn To Be Sung

I will sing and make music to the One.
Psalm 27:6

It took many years of being a rabbi for me to stop feeling shy about singing when leading the congregation. My range is quite limited. I can mostly carry a tune, but get thrown off easily. Singing when I have been alone in desert canyons has helped release some of my inhibitions.

One time, I was by a small river that washed through the desert floor, praying in a whisper. In the silence that filled my pauses, I heard the water moving over sand and rocks. It was a beautiful song.

The canyons don't care how you sound, I told myself. *Join in.* And I did.

It was *Rosh Chodesh*—the first day of a new month—when it is traditional to sing Psalms 113-118, verses of praise and gratitude called *Hallel.*

Hesitantly at first, and then with great enthusiasm, I sang out the words to these psalms in one of their traditional melodies. I felt joyous as I did.

Now I sing psalms all the time. The music's vibrations add such power and beauty.

Find psalm verses that speak to you and sing them. Create your own melodies or put them to tunes you already know. There is no right or wrong way to do this.

One year, a retreat-goer realized that the Hebrew words for Psalm 118:24 fit perfectly into a melody famously sung by Elvis. She had us replace the lyrics: *Wise men say only fools rush in, but I can't help falling in love with you.* with *zeh hayom asah Adonai, nagilah v'nismecha vo* (This is the day that God has made, let us rejoice and delight in it.)

Try it.

Sing a new song to the Infinite Presence.
Psalm 96:1

The Psalms await our voices.

Bitachon – Trust

The Infinite Presence is my strength and my shield;
my heart trusts in the One.
Psalm 28:7

At various times in my life, I have experienced a deep abiding sense of trust—in Hebrew, *bitachon*. I have trusted that there is a Mysterious Presence that permeates all life. I have trusted that this Presence is always here, even in times of great difficulty and pain. Many times, I have been able to turn toward this Presence for comfort and guidance, trusting that I will be supported in meeting whatever life brings.

Commit yourself to the path of Unfolding Mystery.
Trust the Infinite Presence,
and guidance will come.
Psalm 37:5

Over the years, my capacity to trust has wavered, but, even faced with loss and tragedy, I have been able to trust that I am held by a force that is mysterious and ever-present. This abiding trust—this *bitachon*—has grounded and steadied me.

The Psalms have been my guide in cultivating *bitachon*. I have sat, walked, and prayed with *bitachon* verses for many years. I have called them out in times of joy and sorrow. I have expressed them with a full believing heart as well as with skepticism and doubt.

So it is disorienting these days to reach for *bitachon* and come away feeling empty. I am so shaken by the state of the world that I often can't seem to find the trust that has supported me for so long.

Still, I repeat the verses every day. As I do, I pray for the willingness to trust in a mystery beyond anything I can see. I pray for the grounded strength *bitachon* brings. I pray that the Psalms will reach into my trembling heart and plant new seeds of trust within me.

I encourage you to find a verse that speaks to you and read it as you begin or end your day. Let it be a support and guide. And when thoughts arise mocking any notion of *bitachon*, call on the strength of the psalmist and cry out:

Bitachon
Deep Abiding Trust

I walk with integrity
and trust the Infinite Mystery.
I will not be shaken.
Psalm 26:1

In the Divine Source I trust;
I will not be afraid.
What can a person do to me?
Psalm 56:12

Trust the Infinite Mystery and do good.
Dwell in the land and be nourished by faith.
Psalm 37:3

I trust in you, Infinite Presence.
I declare,
You are my source.
Psalm 31:15

Those that trust in the Infinite Presence
are surrounded with steadfast love.
Psalm 32:10

Infinite Presence, those that know you
trust you;
you do not forsake anyone who seeks you.
Psalm 9:11

In peace and harmony,
I lie down to sleep
in your Sacred Presence.
I am not alone;
I dwell in trust.
Psalm 4:9

I trust in your abundant love.
My heart rejoices in your expansive presence,
and I will sing into the Unfolding Mystery,
for all the good bestowed.
Psalm 13:6

My heart rejoices,
my soul delights,
my whole being dwells in trust.
Psalm 16:9

A Sentry Guarding My Heart

Recently, when I was dealing with a difficult family situation, I felt paralyzed by fear. I couldn't turn away from the dread and I couldn't shake it.

I called on a verse I reach for often:

> *This I know, Elohim (God, the Source of All) is with me.*
> Psalm 56:10

I repeated it again and again. Soon, I began hurling this verse at the fear with increasing intensity. Not necessarily believing it, not even really paying attention—I just kept saying it.

> *This I know, the Source of All is with me.*

Walking my dog, sitting at the dining room table, driving the car, waiting for a phone call:

> *This I know, the Source of All is with me.*

At some point, after much repetition, I noticed my body beginning to unclench as my mind started to, finally, attend to the psalm. Sometimes the fear would be gone for a while; other times it just softened. But almost always, with enough repetition, the call of the psalm verse became more powerful than the fear.

Saying the verse did not, of course, magically heal the situation, but it did shift my attention, quiet the foreboding and bring moments of calm relief. The verse provided strength and support that helped me respond to the situation in ways that were helpful.

Fear continued to return, but with the psalm's help, it wasn't always the loudest voice.

I give thanks that the family situation was eventually resolved well. And I give thanks to this psalm verse that I continue to call on every day.

Seeking Refuge

You are my refuge,
a tower of strength.
Psalm 61:4

The Psalms urge us to take refuge in the Infinite Presence, to seek shelter and protection in the embrace of Sacred Mystery. The Psalms assure us that we are held by a force that is vast, mysterious and ever present. We are never alone.

The Source of All is our refuge and strength,
our help in times of trouble,
very close.
Psalm 46:2

I cry out to you, Infinite Mystery.
You are my refuge,
my shelter in the land of the living.
Psalm 142:6

The Sacred Mystery is a shield
for all who seek refuge.
Psalm 18:31

Sometimes the Psalms' call to seek refuge feels abstract, distant, even absurd. Oftentimes it is challenged by my mind's insistence that nothing about it makes rational sense.

And still I hear:

After a difficult encounter, or in the midst of reading some
challenging news, I pause with a psalm verse and repeat it
over and over. With enough persistence, the words begin to
hold me, providing a safe harbor in which I can rest.

I close my eyes and imagine I am being sheltered, embraced
by Sacred Mystery. Even when this sensation lasts only a few
moments, I feel calmed and better able to be present and
helpful.

*I look to you, Infinite Presence,
protect my vulnerable soul.
In you, I take refuge.*
Psalm 141:8

When we allow ourselves to find solace, we can be a refuge
for each other.

On the following pages are more verses for seeking refuge.
Find a verse that appeals to you and take it into meditation.
Call a verse aloud in a moment of difficulty or fear.
Lift your eyes to beauty and call out a verse.
Say a verse as you begin or end the day.

Ignore the skepticism of the rational mind and allow yourself to feel your longings.

You may be surprised by the solace and strength you discover.

I take refuge in the shelter of your wings.
Psalm 61:5

Verses for Seeking Refuge

How essential is the flow of Divine Love;
here we take refuge.
Psalm 36:8

Protect me, God,
I take refuge in you.
Psalm 16:1

The Infinite Presence is my stronghold,
my sheltering rock.
Psalm 94:22

Be gracious with me, Source of All, be merciful.
I take refuge in you.
Until danger passes,
I take refuge in your vast embrace.
Psalm 57:2

In the Infinite Presence, I take refuge.
Psalm 11:1

Infinite Presence, Source of All,
in you I take refuge.
Save me from all that pursues me.
Psalm 7:2

It is better to take refuge in Infinite Mystery
than to trust in wealth.
Psalm 118:9

The Infinite Presence is my rock,
my protection, my rescue, my source,
my grounding where I take refuge,
my shield, my champion, my haven.
Psalm 18:3

Trust in the Infinite's presence at all times.
Pour out your heart before the One.
This is our refuge. Selah
Psalm 62:9

Yeshuah
Salvation, Deliverance, Expanse

Rise up, Infinite Mystery,
save us.
Psalm 3:8

I want us to be saved—delivered from destruction and deceit, rescued from forces of greed and cruelty. I want a mighty, transformative power to sweep in and bring expansive healing for Earth and all beings.

The Hebrew word for this is *yeshuah,* which can be translated as *salvation, deliverance,* or *spacious expanse.*

We beseech you, Infinite Presence, save us.
Psalm 118:25

Infinite Presence,
bring us into the expanse.
Psalm 20:10

Help us, Great Mystery,
deliver us with abundant love.
Psalm 109:26

The Psalms' calls for *yeshuah* carry an ancient power that lifts me toward something mysterious and eternal. They break through my mind's protests that such a force can even exist.

I might expect that calling out in this way would make me
feel embarrassed or foolish. But amazingly, it feels so good to
be unabashed in these longings.

> *I call upon you; save us.*
> Psalm 119:146

I cry out for *yeshuah* constantly—in anger, sadness,
and despair, and also with wild, audacious expectation.
Sometimes the call sails forth seemingly without obstacle.
Other times, it falters. Often, just the calling out helps me
feel I am not alone. And sometimes, just for an instant,
pleading for deliverance lifts me into an expanse of
possibility. In a flash, it's gone, but the sensation lingers.

> *I call out to the Source of All,*
> *and the Mystery saves me.*
> Psalm 55:17

The citations for the verse that follow are noted on the side
of the page. I have placed them there so that the verses can
be read individually or as one psalm beseeching the Mystery
to deliver us all to a spacious expanse.

Calling Out For Yeshuah

Show us great love, Infinite Mystery;
save us.   Psalm 85:8

Save us, for turbulent waters are all around.   Psalm 69:2

Deliver us.
The earth and seas trust in you.   Psalm 65:6

Turn, Infinite Presence,
bring us into the expanse for the sake of love.   Psalm 6:5

Turn toward us with mercy.
Give us strength.
Deliver us.   Psalm 86:16

The Infinite Presence
will send expansive deliverance from the heavens.
Love and truth will trample deceit.   Psalm 57:4

We will turn and rejoice in your saving power.
A generous spirit will sustain us.   Psalm 51:14

The Infinite Presence sings through my strength,
and opens the way into the expanse.   Psalm 118:14

49 Psalms Translated In Full

A Few Notes

Titles of Psalms

L'DAVID
Many psalms are titled *l'david*, *A Psalm to David, of David, for David*—referring to King David and indicating that he is the author of these psalms. In Hebrew, the name *David* also means *beloved* and I have chosen to use this word when translating these titles.

L'MENATZEACH
Many psalms include the word *l'menatzeach* in the title, which is often translated as *Conductor* or *Chief Musician*. Within *l'menatzeach* is the word *netzach,* which in Jewish mysticism calls forth *Eternity, Endurance, Vision.*

I have translated the titles that include *l'menatzeach* in these different ways:
To / For the Composer of Eternity
For Endurance
For Vision
For Enduring Strength

SHIR HAMA'A LOT, SHIR LAMA'A LOT:
Song of / for Ascents
Tradition teaches that the 15 psalms titled *A Song of / for Ascents* were sung as pilgrims ascended to the Temple in Jerusalem to make their offerings. It also has been suggested that this title could be a musical notation calling for a rising in the pitch or crescendo of the song.

I have used *A Song of Ascents* and *A Song of Arising* in the titles of these psalms.

CHILDREN OF KORACH

Twelve psalms are attributed to the children of Korach whose story can be found in the Book of Numbers, chapter 16.

*

Selah

This word appears in various places throughout the psalms and is considered untranslatable.

Many believe it is a musical notation for singers and musicians. *Selah* also could be a companion to *amen*: calling forth an enthusiastic exclamation of praise, a lifting up of prayer, a release into mystery. *Selah* can also be experienced as an invitation to pause and notice what is present and calling.

Halleluyah

Oftentimes in the Psalms, *Halleluyah* is written in the Hebrew as *Hallelu-Yah*, with the hyphen creating two words. This is a command form of the word, calling us to actively praise *Yah*, the Infinite Unfolding Mystery, the very breath of all life. For consistency in English, I have used *Halleluyah* (without the hyphen) throughout the translations.

Psalm 1

Fulfilled is the person who refuses to walk
in the ways of corruption and deceit,
who will not stand with those who hurt and destroy,
and will not dwell with anyone who mocks and offends.

Yearn to know the teachings
that come from Infinite Mystery;
meditate upon them day and night.

You will be like a tree planted by streams of water,
whose fruit comes in its time,
whose leaves always find use,
and whose every action succeeds.

As for the wicked,
brittle and broken, the wind will drive them away.
They will not stand in the face of justice.
They will be unable to rise
in the assembly of the righteous and true.

The Infinite Mystery is close to those who strive for good.

The ways of the wicked will perish.

Psalm 3

A Psalm for the Beloved, Fleeing Confusion and Fear

Infinite Mystery, my enemies are many;
they rise up against me.

They shout that there is no help for me,
that I am alone. *Selah*

But you, Infinite Presence, are my shield;
you are my glory.
You lift my head high.

I cry out to you,
and you answer from your holy mountain. *Selah*

When I lie down,
when I sleep,
when I awake,
your support is with me.

I will not be afraid,
even though I am surrounded
by those intent on destruction.

Rise up, Infinite One, save me.
Strike down these enemies;
break the teeth of the wicked.

The Infinite Mystery is the source of deliverance.

May your blessings be upon us all. *Selah*

Psalm 5

To the Composer of Eternity,
A Psalm from the Waters

Please hear my cries,
Infinite One.
Understand the aching of my heart.

Listen to my voice,
my cries for help.
My source, my hope,
it is to you I pray.

As the day begins, hear me, please.
I pour out my prayers
and wait with the dawn.

For you are not a force that stands with tyrants;
cruelty, brutality
do not abide with you.

The arrogant cannot stand firm before your gaze.
You spurn those who use power to destroy.

You cast out deceivers,
and all those filled with bloodthirsty greed.

As for me,
in your abundant love
I will enter your house.
I will lay myself down in your holy presence
in awe.

Infinite One,
please lead me on a righteous path.
There is so much confusion and fear;
make clear my way.

Many are those who are speaking only lies;
their innermost thoughts are filled with treachery.
Their throats are an open grave;
their lips deceive.

Hold them to account.
Let them fall, destroyed by their own counsel.
Cast them out for their many crimes,
for their defilement of life itself.

Let all who seek refuge in you find joy.
Let them sing into the Mystery.
Shelter and protect them.
May all those who insist on love prevail.

Bless our pursuit of justice.
Enfold us in your highest will.
Let your presence be our shield.

Psalm 8

For Endurance, for Vision,
A Psalm of the Beloved

Infinite Mystery, our support,
how glorious is your presence throughout the earth;
how vast your splendor echoing from the heavens.

From the mouths of children,
from the shoots of tender plants,
you have built a foundation of strength
to oppose those who seek destruction,
to assure violence and cruelty cease.

When I behold the infinite sky—
the delicate work of creation, moon and stars
you have patterned—
I wonder:
what are humans that you would be mindful of us?
Who are we that you would take notice?

And yet you made us to shine,
luminous with the possibility of majesty and splendor.
How will we care for the work of your hands?
How will we stand within this vast creation—
with sheep and ox,
with wild creatures of the forest and field,
with birds, fish,
with all who move in the waters?

Infinite Mystery, our support,
how glorious is your presence throughout the earth.

Psalm 11

For Enduring Strength,
To the Beloved

I take refuge in the Infinite Mystery.
How can you say to me,
Take to the mountains like a bird?

For the wicked bend their bows;
they set their arrows on the strings.
They shoot from the shadows,
taking aim at those with a steadfast heart.

When foundations are destroyed,
what can a righteous person do?

The Infinite Mystery is in the sacred palace.
The Infinite Mystery has a throne in the vastness of space.

The eyes of the Mystery search humankind,
seeking the righteous.
And the wicked, who love violence and cruelty,
the Mystery hates.

Traps of scorching fire
will rain upon the wicked,
and a sulfurous wind will be their lot.

For the Infinite Mystery unfolds in justice.
Justice, the Infinite Mystery, loves.
Those with a steadfast heart
will behold the Sacred Presence.

Psalm 12

To the Composer of Eternity
on the Eight String Harp,
a Psalm for the Beloved

Save us, Infinite Presence,
for it seems that the steadfast ones are gone,
that the faithful are vanishing from among us.

Neighbors speak lies to each other.
Their lips slander;
their hearts deceive.

May the Infinite cut off these slandering lips,
and every tongue that speaks with arrogance and scorn.

They say,
But our tongues shall prevail.
With lips such as ours, who can be our master?

I will arise now, the Infinite calls,
because of the groans of the afflicted,
because of the needs of many.
I will help; I will save.
I testify to this.

The words of the Infinite are pure—
silver refined in fire,
purified in earth, sevenfold.

You, Infinite One, keep watch,
guarding from generation to generation,
forever.

All around, the wicked roam
when cruelty is exalted.

Psalm 13

For the Composer of Eternity
A Psalm to the Beloved

How long, Infinite One?
Will you forget me forever?
How long will you hide your presence from me?

How long will my soul be confused,
and my heart filled with constant grief?
How long will my enemies triumph?

See me.
Answer me.

Illuminate my eyes,
or I will sleep the sleep of death.
Tormented, I will stumble.
Anguish will prevail.

Yet, I trust in your steadfast love.
My heart rejoices in your expansive presence.
I will sing into the Infinite Mystery,
for all the good bestowed.

Psalm 14

For the Composer of Eternity,
To the Beloved

The despairing person says in their heart,
There is no God.
Humans are destructive and filled with hate;
there is no one who does good.

The Infinite looks from the heights,
searching humankind to see if there is someone
who has the good sense
to seek the Divine.

They have all turned away;
they have become corrupt.
There is no one who does good,
not even one.

Do they not realize—
those who wreak havoc,
those who devour people as they devour bread—
what happens when they turn away from the One?

They will be seized by terror,
tormented by fright.
For the One is present in every generation,
with all those who seek justice.

In their plot against the poor,
they will be shamed,
for the One offers refuge.

O, that deliverance might come.

When we are returned from captivity,
when the sacred again prevails,
all who struggle will exalt,
all who wrestle will rejoice.

Psalm 15

A Psalm for the Beloved

Infinite Presence, who sojourns in your tent?
Who dwells on your holy mountain?

One who walks with integrity,
who acts for justice,
and speaks truth from their heart.

One who does not slander,
or cause another harm,
and would never cast blame upon a friend.

One who sees and rejects corruption,
and honors those who live with awe.

One who stands by their word,
even when it is difficult,
who gives without expectation,
and does not take advantage of others.

Those who act in this way
will not be shaken.

Psalm 20

To the Composer of Eternity,
A Psalm for the Beloved

May the Divine Presence answer you in times of trouble;
may the Presence keep you safe.

May help come from the holy realms,
support from the sacred.

May the gifts you offer be received with delight. *Selah*

May the Presence be with you in your heart's desires.
May you feel the Divine in all your plans.

We will sing with joy at your triumphs,
and raise a flag in the name of the Source of All.

May you feel the Divine
in the fullness of your longings.

Now I know the expansive power of the One,
strength that comes as an answer
from the holiness of heavens.

Some call on chariots,
some call on horses;
we will remember and call on the name of the One.

All those pursuing violence will collapse and fall,
and those intent on goodness
will rise
again and again.

Divine Presence, save us;
bring us into the expanse.
The One who reigns beyond time and space
answers us in the moment we call.

Psalm 23

A Psalm for the Beloved

The One is my shepherd;
there is nothing I lack.
The One lays me down
in grassy meadows
and leads me to calm waters.

The One renews my life,
leading me on paths of justice,
for the sake of all.

Though I walk through valleys
in the shadow of death,
I am not afraid,
for you are with me.

Your rod and your staff comfort me.

You spread a table before me
in the presence of all I fear.

You anoint my head with oil;
my cup overflows.

May goodness and love pursue me
all the days of my life.
And I will dwell in the heart of the Sacred
for long and full years.

Psalm 24

For the Beloved, a Psalm

The earth and all that fills it,
the world and all who dwell,
belong to Infinite Mystery.

The Infinite founded it upon the waters,
established it upon flowing rivers.

Infinite One, who can ascend your holy mountain?
Who can stand in your sacred place?
Those with clean hands and a pure heart,
who do not lift up falsehood
and will not abide deceit,
those who raise up blessings from the Infinite Mystery
and justice from the Source of Deliverance.

This is the circle of those who seek you,
who search for your presence. *Selah*

Lift up your heads, O gates.
Rise up, Doorways of Eternity.
The Source of Glory enters.

Who is the Source of Glory?
The Infinite Presence, strong and mighty,
a warrior for battle.

Lift up your heads, O gates,
Rise up, Doorways of Eternity,
the Source of Glory enters.

Who is the Source of Glory?
The Infinite Presence,
the One that contains multitudes,
this is the Source of Glory. *Selah*

Psalm 25

To you, Infinite Presence, I lift my soul.
In You I trust.
May I not be ashamed;
may fear not triumph.

May all who put their hope in you be not ashamed.
May those who act with treachery be disgraced
and left empty.

Help me know your ways.
Teach me your paths.

Guide me with eternal truths;
teach me.
You are the source of possibility.
Every day, with hope, I wait for you.

Remember, your compassion,
your steadfast love,
are always and forever.

Help me not be bound by regret.
See me with love;
see your good in me.

You direct us toward the good,
guiding us if we stray.

And when we feel weak,
you lead us on paths of justice,
teaching us how to find our way.

The paths of Infinite Mystery are love and truth;
bear witness and guard this covenant.

For the sake of life itself,
forgive my transgressions.
My guilt is so great.

Those who live with awe
know which paths to choose.
Their souls abide in goodness;
their seeds fill the earth.

Secrets of Infinite Mystery
are with those in awe.
Through them the sacred covenant
is made known.

Always, I return my eyes to the Presence.
Please release my feet from their traps.

Turn to me.
Have mercy.
I am alone and afraid.

The anguish of my heart swells;
bring me out of affliction and pain.

See my suffering.
Lift guilt from my soul.

See my overwhelming fears,
how they threaten and grow.

Guard and protect me.
Let me not be mired in shame.
I seek refuge in you.

May integrity and decency
watch over me,
for in you I hope.

O God,
save us from all our troubles.

Psalm 26

To the Beloved

Infinite Presence, take notice of me.
I have walked with integrity.
I have trusted in your unfolding mystery.
I have not wavered.

Examine me, test me,
refine my heart, my innermost thoughts,
for your generous love is before my eyes,
and I walk in your truths.

I will not dwell with those who deceive,
or involve myself with hypocrites.
I will not gather with those who do evil,
or sit with those who hurt and destroy.

I wash my hands clean
and circle round your altars.
Let my voice be heard,
speaking gratitude,
relating wonders.

Infinite One,
sheltered with you,
in your glorious presence,
I love.

Do not let me be swept away by those who do harm,
by those disdainful of life,
by those deceptive down to their fingertips,
who use their power to betray.

I will walk with integrity.
Help me. Have mercy.

My feet are on solid ground.
In all gatherings, I will offer blessings
into the Infinite Unfolding.

Psalm 27

To the Beloved

The Infinite Presence is my light and expanse;
whom should I fear?
The Infinite Presence is the strength of my life;
whom should I dread?

When forces come close, threatening to devour me,
When contention appears,
and adversaries attack,
all that is menacing stumbles and falls.

Even as an army of doubt besieges me,
my heart does not fear.
Even as conflict assails me,
I still have trust.

One thing I ask of the Infinite,
one thing I seek:
to dwell in the Presence all the days of my life,
to awaken to the beauty of each moment
as I pass through this world.

The Infinite shelters me as I encounter difficulty and pain.
The Infinite holds me close in deep and hidden places
and lifts me high upon a rock.

Now I can see through to what is true,
and I will offer joyous shouts.
I will sing and make music to the Infinite.

Please, Infinite One, listen to my voice, hear my cry.
Be gracious with me.
Answer me.

You call to my heart, *Seek my presence*;
your presence I seek.

Please do not hide from me;
please do not let me turn away in anger.
You are my help.
Do not let me feel abandoned.
In You, I am safe.

For my mother and father have left me,
and it is you who gathers me in.

Teach me Your ways.
Guide me on paths of integrity;
there is so much to lead me astray.

Don't let me give in to torment and fear,
to lies, illusions and menacing threats.

If only I had the faith to see the goodness of the Infinite
in the land of life.

Cultivate hope in the Infinite Presence.
Let your heart be strong and filled with courage.
Cultivate hope.

Psalm 27 escorts us to the Jewish New Year. It is traditional to say
this Psalm each day from the beginning of the month of *Elul*
through the end of *Sukkot*.

Psalm 29

A Psalm for the Beloved

Give yourselves to Infinite Mystery;
you are children of the Source.

Give yourselves to Mystery, to its glory and its might.

Bow into the sacred presence.
Lay yourselves down in holy splendor.

The voice of Mystery is upon the waters.
The source of glory thunders.
The voice of Mystery is upon the mighty seas.

The voice of Mystery is strength.
The voice of Mystery is splendor.

The voice of Mystery calls though the quaking trees
and the shattering of mighty branches.

The voice of Mystery shakes the mountains;
the peaks tremble.

The voice of Mystery sets fires blazing.

The voice of Mystery quakes the wilderness;
the sacred wilderness shudders.

The voice of Mystery frightens the expectant deer
and rages through the forest,
while all in the Temple shout: *Glory!*

The Infinite Mystery dwells in the deluge.
The Infinite Mystery dwells forever.

Please, Infinite Mystery, give us strength.
Please, Infinite Mystery, bless us with peace.

Psalm 30

A Psalm, a Song of Dedication for the Sacred House,
For the Beloved

I raise you high, Infinite One,
because you have drawn me up
and have not let my enemies rejoice over me.

Infinite One, my Source,
I cried out to you
and you healed me.

You raised me up from the tormenting grave.
You gave me life,
even as I descended into the pit.

Make music to the Infinite, you devout ones.
Give thanks for memories of holiness.

Divine anger passes in a moment.
Divine will is intent on life.

In the evening I lay down weeping,
then dawn brings songs of joy.

I have said in my serenity,
I will never be shaken.

Infinite One, it is by your will
that I stand strong as a mountain.
When your presence is hidden,
I become confused.

I call out to you, Infinite One,
to you I plead for compassion.

What is gained by my demise?
By my descent into the pit?

Will dust acknowledge you?
Will dust declare your truths?

Hear me, please, Infinite One,
Be gracious with me.
Infinite One, please be my help.

You turned my mourning into dancing.
You loosened my grief and clothed me in delight,
so that my whole being
would sing songs of praise
and not be silent.

Infinite One, my Source,
forever I will thank you.

Psalm 31

To the Composer of Eternity,
A Psalm for the Beloved

In You, Divine Presence, I take refuge.
Help me not be concealed in shame.
In your beneficence, free me.

Hear me.
Rescue me quickly.
Be my rock, my strength, my stronghold;
save me.
You are my rock, my protection.
For the sake of all that is,
lead and guide me.

Free me from hidden traps.
You are my strength.

Into your hand I place my spirit.
You redeem me, Infinite One, Source of truths.

I find myself hating those who lie and deceive,
and I turn to you, Divine Presence.
In you I trust.

I rejoice,
I brighten in your steadfast love.
You see my suffering.
You know the distress of my soul.

You do not let me be captured by hatred and fear.
You place my feet on solid ground.

Have mercy on me, Sacred Presence,
I am in great distress,
my eyes worn out by anger,
my soul and body
exhausted by despair.

My life is filled with sorrows.
The years sigh.
All I have done wrong consumes my strength;
my bones waste away.

I am tormented,
filled with reproach.
I have become frightening to all who know me.
They see me and flee.

I have been forgotten;
my heart is deadened.
I am an object,
lost and broken.

I hear the lies of so many.
Terror surrounds me,
so much conspiring to destroy my soul.

But I trust in you, Divine Presence;
you are my source.
My every moment is in your hand.
Save me from torment and dread.

Shine the light of your presence upon me.
With kindness, with love, rescue me.

Please, Divine Presence,
do not let me be ashamed for calling upon you.
Let the evildoers know shame;
let them go down to the silence of the grave.

Let lying lips be quieted.
Let those who speak with arrogance and contempt
be stilled.

How abundant is the good,
even when it is hidden.
In fear and awe, we take refuge in you.

You hold us in the shelter of your presence.
You protect us
from all those who conspire to deceive and destroy.

Blessed is the Divine Presence,
wondrous and steadfast with love,
even as we are under siege.

In fear, in wild panic, I said,
I am cut off and alone.
But you hear my voice,
my pleas, my desperate cries for help.

In your presence I hear:
Love into the Unfolding Mystery.
Be faithful. Keep watch.
The arrogant won't find peace.

Be strong and let your hearts take courage.
Expect the Divine Presence.

Psalm 43

O God, align me with justice.
Help us contend with a nation lost and unkind.
Deliver us from cruel and treacherous leaders.

For you, God, are my strength.

Why do I feel abandoned?
Why do I walk in gloom,
oppressed and afraid?

Send forth your light and truth,
they will guide me.
They will bring me to your holy mountain,
to your sacred presence.

I will come to your altar with gladness, with joy.
With music, I will give thanks to you,
O God, my God.

Why so downcast, my soul,
why so troubled?
Wait. Expect the Divine.

I will again give thanks to God,
the source of ever-present help,
my God.

Psalm 46

To the Composer of Eternity
From the Children of Korach,
A Song of the Hidden Realms

God, you are our refuge and strength,
our help in times of trouble,
very close.

Therefore, we won't be afraid when the earth shakes
and mountains collapse into the heart of the sea,
when waters rage,
and mountains quake in the swells. *Selah*

There is a river whose streams
bring joy and gladness to the cities,
to the sacred dwelling of the Most High.

God is in our midst;
we won't be shaken.
God will help us meet the dawn.

Nations rage, kingdoms topple.
The voice goes forth and the earth dissolves.

The Source of Infinite Possibilities is with us.
This is our refuge and strength. *Selah*

Come and see all that unfolds:
desolation on earth.

The Infinite will cause wars to cease
to the very ends of the land,
breaking bows,
splintering spears,
burning chariots in fire.

Be still and know that I am God.
I am above the nations.
I am above the earth.

The Source of Infinite Possibilities is with us.
This is our refuge and strength. *Selah*

Psalm 50

A Psalm of Gathering

The Infinite Presence, the Source of All, spoke,
calling out to the ends of earth,
from the rising of the sun to its setting.

Appearing in beauty,
shining,
the Source comes
and will not be silent.

In consuming fire,
in wild turbulence,
the Source summons the heavens and earth.
People must be held accountable:

Gather, all who are faithful,
all who have made a covenant
with offerings and sacrifice.

The heavens declare the power of justice.
The Source demands it. *Selah*

Listen my people and I will speak.
I will bear witness.
I am the Source of All.

Daily, you bring me your sacrifices, your offerings.
I do not ask for the bulls from your homes
or the sheep from your flocks,
for every animal of the forest,
every animal of a thousand mountains
is already mine.

I know every bird of the hills.
Every creature of the field
is already with me.

If I were hungry, I would not call upon you,
for I am the world and all that fills it.
Do you think I eat the flesh of bulls
or drink the blood of your male goats?

This is what I ask of you:
Offer gratitude.
Fulfill your vows.
Call on me in times of trouble,
and I will help you.
This will honor me.

The Source says to the wicked,
Who are you to recite my laws
and claim my covenant,
while with hatred
you fling aside my words?

You see a thief
and run with them.
You keep company with those who betray.
You devote your mouth to evil;
you harness your tongue to deceit.

You sit and slander your brother;
you malign your mother's son.

You did all this and heard my silence
and thought I was just like you.
But I rebuke you,
and place these transgressions before your eyes.

Understand this,
all who have forgotten that you are not gods,
lest you be torn apart with no one to save you:

Make sacrifices to honor the sacred.
Offer gratitude.
Align yourself on this path
and I will show you the healing expanse.

Psalm 61

To the Composer of Eternity,
Upon String Instruments
For the Beloved

Hear my shout, Source of All, please listen to my prayer.
I call to you from the edge of earth,
from a heart vulnerable and raw.

Lead me to a rock that is too high for me to reach alone,
for you are my refuge,
a tower of strength in the face of treachery and fear.

I dwell in your tent, hidden in mystery.
I take refuge in the shelter of your wings. *Selah*

You hear my vows.
You give an inheritance to those who are in awe.

May the days of justice and compassion increase
from generation, to generation, to generation.

I sit with the mystery in the presence of the One.
Love and truth stand guard.

Yes, I will sing to all that is, with all that I am.
I will make whole my vows each day.

Psalm 62

To the Composer of Eternity,
A Psalm for the Beloved

 Truly, my soul waits silently for God.
My deliverance comes from the Source.

Truly, God is my rock, my rescue, my haven;
I will not be shaken.

How long will we attack and maim,
toppling others,
knocking them down like a leaning fence?

How long will we take pleasure in deceit,
saying blessings with our mouths,
while inwardly we curse? *Selah*

Truly, wait silently for God, my soul.
The Source of All is my hope.
God is my rock, my rescue, my haven,
I will not be shaken.

From God comes deliverance and glory.
God is my rock of strength,
my refuge.

Trust in God's presence at all times.
Pour out your heart before the One.
This is our refuge. *Selah*

Humans pass like a breath;
our power is an illusion.
We are as vapor.

Do not trust violence.
Have no faith in theft.
Even if force bears fruit,
do not set your heart upon it.

One thing God has spoken,
two things I have heard:
>Strength comes from God.
>God is the source of abundant love.
>A person is made whole through their deeds.

Psalm 63

A Psalm of the Beloved
In the Wilderness

Source of All, you are my God.

I search for you in the shadows of dawn.
My soul thirsts for you;
my body yearns for you
in a dry and weary land without water.

Yes, I will behold the sacred;
I will see your strength and glory.
Your steadfast love is life.
My lips will sing praise.

Yes, I will offer blessings with my life.
I will lift my hands to your presence.

With rich abundance, my soul is full.
My mouth shouts joyful praise.

In the watches of the night, I reflect on you.
I remember your presence.
You are my help,
and in the shadow of your wings, I sing with joy.

My whole being cleaves to you;
your strength supports me.

May those who seek to destroy
plunge to the depths of earth.
May they be felled by the sword;
may they be prey to jackals.

Those aligned with the good will rejoice.
Those dedicated to the Source will praise.
The mouths of deceivers will speak no more.

Psalm 65

To the Composer of Eternity,
A Psalm for the Beloved,
A Song

To you, Source of All, silence is praise.
To you, we make whole our vows.

We come to you, Divine Source.
You listen to our prayers.

When our transgressions overwhelm us,
you forgive.

Blessed are we as we choose to draw close
and dwell in your sacred presence.
May we be filled with the goodness of your house,
your holy sanctuary.

Creator of All, answer us with justice.
Deliver us.
The ends of earth and distant seas
trust in you.

Your strength forms mountains.
You are fortified with might.
You calm the raging seas and quiet the roar of waves.
You soothe the tumult of nations.

From the ends of earth, we see your signs and dwell in awe.
The light of dawn and the darkness of night shout in joy.

You visit the land,
enriching it with waters.
Rivers flow to fullness.

You formed the ground for nourishment.
You prepare our sustenance.

Water flows from the ridges of hills.
You soften the land with showers
and bless sprouting new growth.

You crown the year with goodness;
your paths are ripe with abundance.

Pastures and deserts are filled with plenty.
Hills are girded with joy.

Meadows are clothed with flocks of sheep.
Valleys are covered with grain.
They raise a joyful shout;
they even sing.

Psalm 67

To the Composer of Eternity
Upon Stringed Instruments,
A Psalm, a Song

May the Source of All be gracious with us,
and may we be blessed.
May the Divine Presence shine through us, *Selah,*
so paths of sacred goodness
are known by all throughout the land.

Let it be, that all people will offer praise.
We will offer such thanks and praise.

People will sing with joy, filled with delight,
for justice will fill the land;
steadfast clarity will guide us all. *Selah*

Let it be, that all people will offer praise.
We will offer such thanks and praise.

Bless us, Divine Source,
with earth's abundant generosity.
Bless us to the ends of earth
with wonder, with awe.

Psalm 71

In you, Infinite Presence,
I take refuge.
May I never be ashamed.

Through your beneficence, deliver me,
rescue me,
reach for me,
free me.

Be for me a sheltering rock
that I can always come to.

You call forth my salvation.
You are my rock, my support.

Please, rescue me from the hands of wickedness,
from the grasp of cruelty and violence.

You are my hope.
Trusting you is my foundation.

I have relied on you from birth.
You drew me from my mother's womb.
I sing praises to you
always.

Make me a sign for many
that you are a refuge of strength.

My mouth is filled with praise.
All day I speak of your radiance.

Do not cast me out in old age.
When I have no strength,
do not forsake me.

Dreadful thoughts attack me.
They insist I've been abandoned by God.
Vile images pursue me,
claiming there is no one who will come to my rescue.

Please God, be not far from me.
Rush to my help.
May deceivers perish in shame.
May tormentors be consumed by scorn and disgrace.

As for me,
I will wait hopefully for your presence always,
and I will increase my praise.

All day I will speak of your beneficence,
of your mighty expansive force.

Even with all I do not know,
I will come with the strength of your presence,
and remember that you are the source of justice.

Long ago you taught me
to speak of wonders.

As I become old and gray,
do not abandon me.
Let me speak about you to the generations,
declaring your strength to those who will come.

Your justice
reaches the high expanse.
Do great things, Source of All,
for who is like you?

You are with us in affliction,
in anguish and pain.
You return us to life,
raising us up from the depths.

You increase our greatness;
you turn and bring comfort.

I will give thanks to you on the harp,
singing of your faithful presence.

My lips will shout in jubilation.
My soul will sing to you.

All day I will speak of your justice
and place it upon my heart.

Those seeking destruction and ruin
will perish in shameful disgrace.

Psalm 82

A Psalm of Gathering

God stands in the Divine assembly,
in the midst of all that is sacred,
and calls us to judgment.

How long will dishonesty rule?
How long will favor be shown to the wicked?

Justice must be done.
Rescue the poor, the vulnerable, all those in need.
Save us from the hands of tyrants.

Save us from those who act without conscience,
who walk in the shadows of darkness.
The very foundation of earth shakes.

You think you are gods,
beings from on high,
but you will perish as humans do.
You will fall.

Arise, Divine Mystery, show us justice.
Let this be our inheritance.

Psalm 84

To the Composer of Eternity
Upon Musical Instruments,
From the Children of Korach,
A Psalm

Divine Mystery, Source of Possibility,
how beloved are your dwelling places.

My soul languishes, longing to draw close.
My heart, my body, yearn to shout with joy
to you, the Source of Life.

Even the bird has found a home,
and the sparrow a nest for her young.
They draw close to your sacred presence,
O Source of Infinite Possibility,
my God.

Content are those who dwell
at home in your presence.
Their very being offers praise. *Selah*

Content are those whose strength is in you.
They find you in the channels of their hearts.

They pass through a valley of tears
and make it a wellspring.
Soft rain envelops it with blessing.

They go from strength to strength,
seen by the Source of All.

Divine Mystery, Source of Possibility,
hear my prayers.
Listen, you who come through the ancestors. *Selah*

Look upon our shields;
see our faces.
Better is one day in your courtyard
than thousands away from you.

I would rather stand vulnerable at the edge of your house
than find shelter among the arrogant.

The Divine Mystery
is sun and shield.
From Mystery comes grace and glory.
Goodness is not withheld
from those who walk with integrity.

Divine Mystery, Source of Possibility,
blessed is the person who trusts in you.

Psalm 91

O you who dwell in the shelter of the Most High,
resting in the shadow of divine embrace,
I say to Infinite Mystery,
You are my refuge, my strength;
I trust in you.

The Mystery will deliver us from hunter's traps,
from plagues of destruction and fear.

The Mystery will hold us close.
We will find refuge in the wings of the Divine,
protection in truth.

We don't have to be afraid of terrors of the night,
or arrows that fly by day.
We don't have to fear plagues that stalk the darkness
or destruction that rages at noon.

Thousands and thousands will fall
and we will not be moved.
We will see with our own eyes
the reckoning of the wicked.

Infinite Mystery is our refuge,
the Most High our haven.
Evil will not topple us;
devastation will not come close.

The Mystery calls angels to guard us on our paths.
They carry us in their hands,
lest we strike our foot against a stone.
They help us walk in danger
among menacing threats.

The Mystery calls,
Your devotion will free you.
You will know me,
and I will lift you up.
When you call on me, I will answer;
I will be with you in distress.
I will rescue you and glorify your presence.

May your days be filled with satisfaction.
May your days touch the Infinite expanse.

Psalm 96

Sing a new song to the Infinite Presence.
Sing to the Presence, all Earth.

Sing to the Infinite Presence and offer blessings.
Every day, sing of expansive mystery.

Tell stories of glory and wonder,
for great is the Infinite Unfolding,
praised with awe,
amid all that is sacred.

False idols will crumble.
Mystery will rise.

Glory and majesty go forth from the Presence.
Strength and beauty create holy ground.

Families and all people,
come into the Presence,
come into the glory and strength of the Divine.

Come and honor the sacred.
Lift up your offerings and draw close to the source.

Lay yourselves down in holy splendor.
Tremble before the One, all Earth.

Declare among nations:
Infinite Mystery reigns.

The world stands firm;
it will not be shaken.
Justice will come
with equity,
with firmness.

Let the heavens rejoice,
let the earth delight,
let the sea in its fullness roar.

Let fields and all that grows celebrate;
let trees in the forests sing with joy
before the Sacred Presence,
for the Infinite Mystery is coming
to bring justice for earth and all people—
justice that is faithful,
justice that is true.

Psalm 100

A Psalm of Thanksgiving

Raise a joyful shout to the Infinite Presence,
all who dwell on earth.
Come before the Presence with delight.
Serve in joy.

Know that the Infinite is the Source of All.
We have been made by the Infinite,
and we are the flock the Infinite tends.

Enter the gates with gratitude.
Draw close with praise.
Give thanks,
offer blessings,
for goodness unfolds in mystery.

Love expands from generation to generation.
The Infinite Presence is forever faithful.

Psalm 111

Halleluyah
Offer Praise

With all my heart, I give thanks into the Unfolding Mystery.
In the secret places of my soul
and in the midst of sacred community,
I give thanks.

Great are the ways of Mystery;
seekers will delight in them.

Glory and splendor fill creation.
Divine beneficence stands forever.

Let us be aware of wonders;
grace and compassion flow from Mystery.
Sustenance comes through awe.
Forever and always is our covenant with the One.

The power of the Mystery has been shown to the people,
a mighty stream to the nations.

The handiwork of the Mystery is truth and justice.
The teachings are faithful.
Established with clarity and truth,
they stand forever.

The Mystery sends redemption to the people
and calls forth a covenant that is sacred,
wondrous and eternal.

The beginning of wisdom is awe of the Unfolding Mystery.
Good sense comes to all who practice.
Praise stands forever.

Psalm 112

Halleluyah
Offer Praise

Ashrei—fulfilled—are those in awe of Infinite Mystery,
who passionately act for the good of all.
Their seeds will grow with mighty strength.
Generations will be blessed by their integrity.

Abundance fills their homes;
their beneficence stands forever.
Lights shine through them in darkness;
lights of graciousness, compassion and justice shine.

Blessed are those who act with grace and generosity,
who strive for fairness with words and deeds;
they will not be shaken.
Their acts of justice will unfold forever.

They will not be afraid when evil comes.
Their hearts are firm;
they trust in Infinite Mystery.

With hearts supported by the Infinite,
they will not be frightened.
They will watch as tyrants fall.

They share their abundance with those in need.
Their beneficence stands forever.
Lights of glory shine through them.

The wicked will see this and be grieved.
They will gnash their teeth.
Their courage will fail.
All their plans will perish.

Psalm 113

Halleluyah
All who long to be of service offer praise.
Praise the Infinite Mystery.
Let the Infinite be blessed, now and forever.
From the rising of the sun to its setting,
offer praise.

Beyond the reach of human design is Infinite Mystery,
shining in glory.
Who is this One—the Mystery we call God—
dwelling in eternity and here on earth?
God is the One raising the weak up from the dust,
lifting up those discarded as waste,
seating them with dignity among the generous and noble,
transforming the desolate home
into a dwelling filled with fruitful joy.

Halleluyah
Offer Praise

In Jewish liturgy Psalms 113-118 comprise *Hallel*, offerings
of praise and gratitude recited in full or in part on the first day
of every Jewish month and during Passover, Sukkot, Shavuot
and the eight days of Chanukah.

Psalm 114

When Israel went from the narrow place,
out of constriction and fear,
they became a sacred dwelling.

The sea saw and fled;
the Jordan River flowed backward.
The mountains skipped like rams,
the hills like young sheep.

What is happening to you, Sea, that you flee?
To you, Jordan River, that you turn back?
To you, Mountains, that you skip like rams?
And to you, Hills, that you become like young sheep?

The earth trembles at the presence of Mystery.
All life trembles at the Mystery
that turns rocks into pools of water,
flint into flowing fountains.

Psalm 115

Not for our sake, Infinite Mystery, for the sake of all—
for the sake of love and truth—
bring honor and glory.

So many say, *Where is God?*
God is in the far reaches of mystery,
unfolding in desire and deeds.

Sorrows come as we worship silver and gold,
grief as we grasp for power.

Suddenly,
our mouths cannot speak,
our eyes cannot see,
our ears are unable to listen.

Our noses cannot smell,
our hands cannot feel,
our feet are unable to walk,
our throats do not utter a sound.

We have created a sham,
trusted in lies.
We have become what we worship.

Let us wrestle and trust in Mystery.
This is our help and our shield.

Let us seek peace and trust in Mystery.
This is our help and our shield.

Let us cultivate awe and trust in Mystery.
This is our help and our shield.

The Infinite Mystery is mindful of us
and offers blessings as we struggle,
as we seek,
as we question and grow.

May the Mystery increase the blessings
that come through us all.
May we be blessed by the One
that fills the heavens and earth.

The heavens belong to the Infinite,
and the earth has been given to humankind.
Not giving thanks deadens the body;
unwillingness to praise dampens the spirit.

Let us bend our knees and bow.
Let us offer blessings into the Infinite Mystery,
now and always.
Halleluyah

Psalm 116

I love,
because the Infinite Presence hears my voice
and listens to my pleas.
Whenever I call,
the Presence is there.

Cords of death ensnared me;
torments took hold.
Filled with anguish and sorrow,
I called on the Presence:
Please rescue me.

The Infinite Presence is generosity and beneficence.
Our Source is compassion.

The Presence protects us.
I was brought low,
and the Presence was there.

Return, my soul;
rest in the embrace of Infinite care.

You have delivered my soul from numbing despair,
my eyes from weeping,
my feet from stumbling.

I will walk in the presence of the One in the lands of life.
I will be faithful.

Out of great suffering, I have said:
All humans deceive.

How can I return to the Presence,
to the goodness bestowed?

I will raise the cup of possibility
and call on the name of the One.

I will make whole my vows
in the presence of all.

Sorrowful in the eyes of the One
is the death of generosity and love.

Please, Infinite Presence, I long to serve.
You have loosened the cords that bind me.

To You, I make offerings of gratitude,
and in the name of the Infinite Presence, I cry out.

I will make whole my vows
in the presence of all,
in the courtyards of the Infinite,
in the midst of cities yearning for peace.

Halleluyah
Offer Praise

Psalm 117

Praise the Infinite Unfolding, all nations.
Celebrate the Great Mystery, all people.

For the might of Divine love is upon us,
and the faith of the Mystery is forever.

Halleluyah
Offer Praise

Psalm 118

Let us give thanks to the Infinite Mystery for all the good,
for love and kindness are forever.
Let all who wrestle say,
Love and kindness are forever.
Let all who seek peace say,
Love and kindness are forever.
Let all who live in awe say,
Love and kindness are forever.

From the narrow place, I called out to the Mystery,
and I was answered with expansiveness.

The Infinite is with me; I will not be afraid.
What can a person do to me?
The Infinite is my help;
I can face hatred and fear.

It is better to take refuge in Mystery
than to trust in humankind.
It is better to take refuge in Mystery
than to trust in wealth.

Nations assail me.
In the name of the Infinite,
I will seek their hearts.

They surround and assail me.
In the name of the Infinite,
I will seek their hearts.

They assail me like bees,
like fiery thorns.
In the name of the Infinite,
I will seek their hearts.

I was pushed hard,
I nearly fell,
but the Infinite was my help.

The song of Infinite Mystery is my strength,
and opens the way into the expanse.

A joyful, triumphant cry
resounds from those seeking justice.

The strength of the Infinite is courage.
The strength of the Infinite is raised up.
The strength of the Infinite is courage.

I shall not die, but live,
and speak of the Infinite Unfolding.

I have faced hardship and pain
but have not given up.

Open for me the gates of justice,
I will enter and give thanks.
This is the gateway to Infinite Mystery.
Let all those seeking justice come in.

I will give thanks for the ways you have answered me,
and brought me into the expanse.
The stone the builders rejected
has become the cornerstone.
All unfolds from Mystery,
and is wondrous in our sight.
This is the moment the Infinite has made;
let us rejoice and delight in it.

Please save us, Infinite Mystery, we beseech you.
Please help us thrive, Infinite Mystery, we beseech you.

Blessed are those who enter in the name of the One.
We bless you from the home of the One.

Light shines from the Infinite expanse.
Let us weave the festival offerings
to the radiance of the altar.

You are my Source and I thank you.
You are my Source and I raise you up.

Let us give thanks to the Infinite Mystery for all the good;
for love and kindness are forever.

Psalm 120

A Song of Ascents

In constriction and pain,
I called out to the One
and was answered.

Save me from lying lips
and treacherous tongues.
Who benefits from this deceit?
Lies become sharpened arrows,
hot coals, burning wood.

Too long have I wandered;
too long have I dwelled
with those who hate peace.

I am for peace,
but when I speak,
they raise the call for war.

Psalm 121

A Song of Ascents

I lift my eyes to the mountains;
from where does my help come?
My help comes from the Infinite Presence,
revealed in the heavens and earth.

The Presence holds us steady and guards us always.

Take notice:
the Infinite Presence doesn't slumber, doesn't sleep.

The Presence is with us in the shadows and by our side.
The Presence protects us through the light of day
and the darkness of night.

The Presence guards us from all evil,
and protects the life-breath of our souls.

The Infinite Presence guards our going out and coming in,
now and always.

Psalm 126

A Song of Arising

When the Infinite Mystery returns us from captivity
we will be like dreamers.
Our mouths will be filled with laughter,
our tongues with joyous songs.

The nations will declare,
Greatness comes from Mystery.

The Mystery will lift us
and together we will rejoice.

Return us from captivity, Infinite Mystery;
return us like springs in the desert.

We who sow in tears
will reap in joyous celebration.

We who walk along weeping,
carrying bags of seeds,
will surely return in celebration,
lifting up all that has grown.

Psalm 130

A Song of Ascents

Out of the depths I cry out to you, Infinite Mystery.
Please hear my voice.
Please listen to my pleas.
If we were only our misdeeds, who could possibly stand?
With you is forgiveness,
and we are in awe.

I hope into the Unfolding Mystery.
With all my being,
I hope
and wait for a sign.

My soul longs for you
like those who watch through the night,
waiting for dawn,
like those who wait and watch for the dawn.

Let us wait and hope.
In the Unfolding Mystery is infinite love.
In the Unfolding Mystery is possibility and rescue.
The Unfolding Mystery will release us from guilt and regret.

Between Rosh Hashanah and Yom Kippur, it is traditional to say
Psalm 130 each day to support and inspire *teshuvah*—turning toward
healing, forgiveness and repair.

Psalm 134

A Song of Ascents

Arise,
and offer blessings into the Infinite Mystery.
All who serve the Mystery,
all who stand in the Sacred Presence
in the darkness of night,
lift your hands toward holiness and offer blessings.

And may the Infinite Mystery that fills heaven and earth
bless you.

Psalm 138

To the Beloved

I give thanks to you with all my heart.
In relationship with the Source of All, I sing.
I lay myself down in your sacred presence
and offer gratitude for your steadfast love and truths.

How great is the unfolding of creation.
In the moment I call, you answer me.
You inspire my soul with strength.

Let those who think they rule the earth
acknowledge your Infinite Presence.
Let them hear the sacred stirring;
let them sing of paths of mystery,
for glorious is the Presence.

Those laid low are noticed,
and those held at a distance
are brought close.

Even as I walk in the midst of troubles,
you enliven me.
You send forth your expansive strength
to combat adversity and fear.

Infinite Presence, you complete me.
Mysterious and forever is your steadfast love.
Do not let go of the work of your hands.

Psalm 146

Praise the Infinite Mystery, my soul.
I praise the Mystery with my life.
I sing to the Source with all that I am.

Do not put your trust in rulers:
they are only human
and cannot alone bring salvation.

Their breath departs,
they return to earth,
their plans perish.

Content are those who turn to the Source for help,
whose hope is the Mystery that fills heaven and earth,
the seas and all within them.
The Mystery is forever faithful and true.

The Infinite Mystery brings justice to the oppressed,
gives bread to the hungry,
releases those who are bound.

The Mystery opens our eyes,
stands us upright,
and sends love into the pursuit of justice.

The Mystery guards the vulnerable,
gives them strength,
and subverts the path of the wicked.

The Infinite Mystery reigns forever,
the Source of All, from generation to generation.

Halleluyah
Offer Praise

Psalm 148

Halleluyah
Praise the Infinite Unfolding Mystery.

Praise the Mystery from the heavens.
Praise the Mystery from the heights.
Offer praise, all you Divine messengers.
Offer praise, legions and guides.

Offer praise, sun and moon
and distant, shimmering stars.
Offer praise, expansive sky,
and waters above the heavens.

Offer praise.
All creation unfolds from Mystery
and abides forever.
Order and harmony are the Infinite's design.

Praise the Infinite Unfolding, creatures of earth
and serpents of ocean depths.
Fire and hail, snow and mist, winds and storms—
all come from mystery.

Mountains and hills, fruit trees and forest,
animals of the wild, animals of the fields,
small creatures and soaring birds,
kings and rulers,
judges and princes,
elders and children—all together—
praise the Infinite Unfolding.

Praise the One that unites us,
the majestic splendor of creation.

Rays of light go forth from Mystery,
illuminating our praise,
inspiring our devotion.

Let us draw close and praise the Infinite Unfolding Mystery.
Halleluyah

Psalm 150

Praise the Infinite Mystery.
Praise the Sacred Presence.
Praise the Mystery in the enduring expanse.

Praise the Mystery's mighty acts.
Praise the Mystery's great abundance.

Praise with blasts of the shofar;
praise with the lute and harp.
Praise with timbrels and dance;
praise with strings and flute.
Praise with cymbals and resounding bells.

Let the breath of all life praise the Infinite Mystery.

Halleluyah

Ashrei To Halleluyah

Happy are those who dwell at home in the One;
their very being shouts Halleluyah.
Selah
Psalm 84:5

The Book of Psalms opens with the call *ashrei*, not an easy word to translate. It can be rendered as *happy, blessed, content, praiseworthy, fortunate, fulfilled.*

The Book of Psalms closes with the call *Hallelu-Yah:* Praise *Yah*—God—the Infinite Unfolding of all life. Shout it out: *Hallelu-Yah.*

Amid these two calls, the 150 Psalms cry out in joy and weep in sorrow. They sing with gratitude and tremble with fear. In both harmony and dissonance, they give voice to the fullness of life.

With this opening call of *ashrei*, what are the Psalms guiding us toward?

Two stories:

About twenty years ago, I had the great fortune to take part in Jewish mindfulness retreats in the wilds of Alaska. Delivered by floatplane to a remote island, about twelve of us kayaked and camped for ten days in the company of breaching whales, jumping salmon and sweeping storms. (These amazing journeys were conceived and co-led by Rabbi Rachel Cowan *z'l,* whose vision and efforts transformed Jewish life for so many.)

One afternoon I was walking back to camp with a
companion. We were marveling at the inhabitants of the tide
pools and the sea kelp that grew three feet in one day. All of a
sudden, a sensation of absolute contentment arose within me
and I thought, *If I were to die right here, right now, I would be
completely satisfied. I would leave this world happy. All is well.*

In that instant I thought, *This is ashrei*, a moment of being
so full, so at peace, there is no wanting for anything else. No
yearning, no needing, a sensation of complete fulfillment and
well-being.

The second story:

When my beloved mom was 61, she was diagnosed with Stage
4 lung cancer. My son was less than a year old and we had
been so excited about her becoming Grammy. There weren't
many treatments available, and from the beginning, there was
not much hope of recovery. She died exactly one year after
being diagnosed.

We had a lot of family gatherings that year. One night, seated
around the Shabbat table, we passed around a *mezuzah* we
had bought for my mom. Each of us in turn held it and
gave her a blessing. Mom listened closely and afterwards
exclaimed, with pure joy, "This is perfect—just *perfect*." She
spread her arms wide and repeated again, "*This is perfect*." My
brother, not missing a beat, said, "Mom, this would be perfect
if you didn't have cancer."

Again, I had an experience of *ashrei*. Gratitude and love had burned through grief and worry and delivered us to a moment of fullness and well-being.

Ashrei sings throughout the Psalms. The word appears in the Psalms more than anywhere else in the Hebrew Bible. (26 times) It occurs only once in the Torah (in Deuteronomy, the last of the five books of Moses) and only five times in the books of the Prophets.

The Psalms suggest that *ashrei*—contentment, fulfillment, happiness—is an inner state that we cultivate through our actions and intentions. *Ashrei* comes as we treat each other with dignity, act with integrity, and seek relationship with Divine Mystery. *Ashrei* arises as we dwell in joy and wonder. It flourishes as we feel our connection with each other and all creation. It is strengthened as we call ourselves present, with tenderness and care, to all that life brings.

> *Ashrei are those who guard justice*
> *and seek to act with integrity at all times.*
> Psalm 106:3

> *Ashrei are those who call on your strength,*
> *who set their hearts on sacred pilgrimage.*
> Psalm 84:6

By opening with this call, the Psalms urge us to seek experiences of *ashrei* and cultivate this inner quality in ourselves. We take on this practice not just for our own sake. We seek *ashrei* so that goodness and blessing come forth from our very being. *Halleluyah*

What follows are verses that call forth *ashrei*. You might consider:

Finding a verse that speaks to you, writing it out, and putting it some place where you will see it easily.

Calling out a verse as you begin or end the day.

Meditating on just the word *ashrei*.

Keeping an *ashrei* journal to note moments and experiences of deep contentment and fulfillment.

> *Ashrei are those*
> *who guard their practices*
> *and seek the Infinite Presence*
> *with all their hearts.*
> Psalm 119:2

Ashrei

In these verses, I have not translated the word *ashrei*. You might find it helpful to read them as they are, or to substitute any of the possible translations—*happy, fulfilled, praiseworthy, content, blessed, fortunate.*

Ashrei is the person
who refuses to walk in the ways of corruption and deceit,
who will not stand with those who hurt and destroy,
and will not dwell with anyone who mocks and offends.
Psalm 1:1

Taste and see the goodness of the Unfolding Mystery.
Ashrei is the person who takes refuge here.
Psalm 34:9

Ashrei are those mindful of the poor
and everyone who struggles.
Psalm 41:2

A Song of Arising:
Ashrei are those who live in awe,
and walk in the ways of Infinite Mystery.
Psalm 128:1

Infinite One, source of all possibility,
ashrei is the person who trusts in you.
Psalm 84:13

Ashrei is the person who turns to the Source for help,
who hopes into the Unfolding Mystery.
Psalm 146:5

Ashrei are those
who place their trust in the Infinite Presence
and refuse to align with the arrogant
and those who deceive.
Psalm 40:5

Ashrei are those
who walk with integrity,
their steps aligned with the Infinite.
Psalm 119:1

Halleluyah
Ashrei is the person
in awe of Infinite Mystery,
who passionately acts for the good of all.
Psalm 112:1

Halleluyah

Praise the Mystery, praise the Infinite Presence,
praise the Unfolding of all Life.

The call *Halleluyah* sings throughout the Psalms.
In Psalm 148: 9–13
we hear:

Mountains and hills, fruit trees and forest,
animals of the wild, animals of the fields,
small creatures and soaring birds,
kings and rulers,
judges and princes,
all people of earth,
elders and children,
all together,
praise Yah, the Infinite Unfolding.
Praise the One that unites us,
the majestic splendor of creation.

Trees, mountains, creatures of land, sea and sky offer praise
with their very being. Light shimmering on a mountain lake,
flowers blooming, birds migrating—all are offerings of praise.

Psalms call us to be part of this sacred chorus, to be present to
this glorious, tumultuous world, to be fully alive, here with all
beings in the unfolding of creation—and to shout out praise.

What does it mean to offer praise in a world that is
magnificent, holy, broken and filled with sorrows?

Halleluyah is a shout of aliveness, a song of life unfolding.

There are times when life feels wondrous, filled with joy
and celebration. Standing beneath a blossoming cherry tree,
watching the sky turn pink, orange, and blue at dawn, sharing
moments of connection with family and friends, we feel the
richness of life.

And there are times when this same aliveness feels
excruciating as we face tragedy and loss and witness each
other's suffering.

Praise rises from love, from relationship, from presence.

Halleluyah
I am here.
I will celebrate the abundance of blessings.
I will weep in anguish and pain.
I will not turn away.
I will not separate myself.
I will shout, wail, celebrate, sob and love.

The very last verse in the Book of Psalms calls:

> *Let the breath of all life*
> *praise the Infinite Unfolding Mystery,*
> *Halleluyah*
> Psalm 150:6

May our souls shout in response:
Yes. For the sake of all creation, I will join the holy choir.
My life will be an offering of praise.

Halleluyah

Afterward

It is the beginning of 5786, and I am astounded to have
reached the moment of declaring this book complete—even
as I know I could keep writing and rewriting it *l'olam va'ed*,
forever and ever.

These offerings are a culmination of many years of
exploration and practice. In July 2024 (*Tammuz* 5785)
I began writing and weaving this book together in earnest.
It went through some big changes after November 2024
and I am sure that if I began it today it would be a different
book still.

As the psalmist sings: *I come with the scroll of the book that
is written upon me.*

Psalm 40:8

I pray that it is helpful as we continue to navigate our times.

hazak hazak v'nit'hazek
Let us be strong and courageous.
Let us strengthen each other.

4 *Tishrei* 5786
Erev Shabbat Shuva
26 September 2025

Acknowledgements

I give such thanks:

To Melanie Baise, whose gift in memory of her beloved, Lia Lynn Rosen, helped propel this book into being. Not only did Melanie's gift allow time and space for writing, it created a sacred covenant between us that held me steady and encouraged me on. Melanie and Lia *z"l* helped place generosity and devotion at the foundation of this endeavor.

To Carol Towarnicky, with whom I have been journeying through the psalms for over twenty years. Carol edited these writings with great skill, care, love and humor. Her insights clarified my thinking. Her determination kept me going. Her wise counsel shines in these pages. With Carol I felt I could be completely vulnerable and write with abandon. I still think about some of the early drafts I sent her—I can imagine Carol reading them, shaking her head, taking a deep breath and saying to herself…" *we still have quite a way to go.*" Truly, this book would not be here without her. Forever I give thanks.

To Phyllis Myers, for all the ways she lifts and carries *A Way In* and for all she has done to make sure this book came to be. I am so grateful to have Phyllis by my side. With joy, clarity and skill, Phyl always finds a way for ideas and visions to take root and grow.

To Elise Kraemer and Lance Laver for reading over these pages with love and care.

To the *A Way In* board whose work, dedication, love and faith make all our offerings possible.

To the *A Way In* community: traveling together through the seasons and years is a joy and honor.

Many of my family members who have passed were with me as I wrote this book. I could feel them rooting for me and am grateful to them now and always.

To my friends and family with whom I laugh, cry, sing, dance, wail, celebrate, rage and wonder, thank you for your loving companionship and your generous support.

Much of this book took shape when I was in the Adirondack region of New York. I had the blessing to be there for a few weeks during each season this past year. The waters, sky, trees and creatures of this wild, beautiful land held and inspired me. Time and time again they lifted me beyond confusion and fear and pointed the way forward.

To my beloved partner, Etja, who walked by my side with great love, playful humor and a wellspring of encouragement—*I give thanks to you with all my heart.*

And to the Source of All, the Infinite Unfolding Mystery, I bow to you.

May this offering be for the healing and mending of all the worlds.

Rabbi Yael Levy

For more than two decades, Rabbi Yael Levy has developed a unique approach to Mindfulness that, while deeply rooted in Jewish texts and tradition, has proven meaningful to people of different faiths and paths. She is a founder and the director of *A Way In* Jewish Mindfulness organization and Rabbi Emerita of Mishkan Shalom congregation in Philadelphia, where she served for 28 years.

Rabbi Yael's 2010 guide to Counting the Omer, *Journey through the Wilderness*, helped expand interest in this ancient Jewish practice. *Directing the Heart* (2018) provided Mindfulness Teachings and Practices inspired by the weekly Torah portions. In all her books, classes, online teachings and retreats, Rabbi Yael shares her love of the Psalms.

She is a graduate of the Reconstructionist Rabbinical College and has completed training programs with the Institute for Jewish Spirituality. For four years, she co-led the Institute's Mindfulness retreats in the wilds of Alaska. She is a spiritual director for rabbinical students and in private practice.

An avid hiker and kayaker, all of Rabbi Yael's offerings are informed by a passionate connection to Earth and a deep commitment to the well-being of all life. Named one of "America's Most Inspiring Rabbis" by the Jewish Forward in 2014, her work has been featured in the New York Times, Huffington Post and other publications.

A Way In

A *Way In* Jewish Mindfulness organization shares Rabbi Yael Levy's Mindfulness teachings with people in many parts of the world through weekly writings, Torah study classes and guided meditations. Online classes as well as in-person retreats are offered several times each year.

A Way In's offerings seek to strengthen spiritual practice and, with it, the capacity to meet all that life brings with resilience, faith, courage and compassion. It serves a vibrant online community that includes people of different backgrounds throughout North America, offering support to help us live well for the sake of each other and all the world.